THE EPISTLE OF PAUL
TO THE GALATIANS

An Exposition

THE EPISTLE
OF PAUL
TO
THE GALATIANS

An Exposition

by
CHARLES R. ERDMAN

PREFACE BY EARL F. ZEIGLER

THE WESTMINSTER PRESS

PHILADELPHIA

Published by The Westminster Press
Philadelphia, Pennsylvania

PRINTED IN THE UNITED STATES OF AMERICA

5   6   7   8   9   10

To
all who love liberty
who deplore license
and who
seek to fulfill
the law of Christ

PREFACE

"For freedom Christ has set us free; stand fast therefore, and do not submit again to a yoke of slavery."—*The apostle Paul.*

"Eternal vigilance is the price of liberty."—*Thomas Jefferson.*

The Letter of Paul to the Galatians has been eulogized as the Magna Charta of the Christian faith; the declaration of religious independence; and its author as the Christian of all time who has best understood Jesus Christ. Without doubt both the letter and its author represent a high-water mark in the history of the Christian faith—in the history of all religion, as a matter of fact.

Like many other great writings, it is comparatively brief. Ten double space typewritten pages adding up to about three thousand words, and ten or fifteen cents postage to mail it, would be the modern equivalent. But what words! They flow from the mind of Paul white-hot with passion and logic but tender with compassion for his misguided parishioners. Meddlers without authority from the Jersualem church, or from any of the apostles, had taken it upon themselves to keep the church within Judaism by *permitting* both Gentile and Jewish converts to believe in Jesus as the Messiah, resurrected and ascended, but *compelling* all members to observe the ritual and ceremonials of Judaism. This was not the "gospel" that Jesus had proclaimed, nor the gospel that Paul had preached in Galatia, and to which the converts, both Jew and non-Jew, had professed their faith. The Holy Spirit had given his attestation to this gospel by coming into the lives of the converts. At stake was the future of missionary work throughout the Roman Empire—throughout the world of the future. At stake also was Paul's apostleship. If the Judaizers could discredit his gospel, Paul's mission would become a lost cause.

To do justice to an exposition of so weighty a letter, Dr. Charles R. Erdman was selected. The volume before the reader is the result of his dedicated and scholarly labors. Dr. Erdman had had wide pastoral experience. He had been professor of practical theology in Princeton Theological Seminary for several decades. The General Assembly of the Presbyterian Church in the U.S.A. chose him as its moderator. The missionary work of the church was enriched by his wise leadership and guidance.

When the reader begins to use this volume as a guide to the study of Galatians, he is certain to be impressed, as well as mentally and spiritually enlarged, by the helpful explanations of the text, section by section according to the expositor's illuminating outline. A great amount of research by Biblical scholars has been lavished on this Galatian letter. Dr. Erdman weighs the evidence that has been collected and shares his conclusions in a way that helps the student to reach his own as he comes across statements by Paul that require careful and prayerful consideration. Today's Bible students, as they read Galatians, must accept the responsibility in our generation for preserving and proclaiming the gospel that makes faith in Christ the sole test for the believer's life here and hereafter. We have not yet reached in our churches the height and depth of the freedom of conscience for which Paul so eloquently pleaded. But we must push forward.

EARL F. ZEIGLER

FOREWORD

A fugitive letter, written in the first century to obscure groups of Christians, was destined to become the Magna Charta of spiritual freedom for the whole world and for all time. This epistle to the Galatians forms an essential chapter in the history of the early church. It was a vital cause of the great religious movement which dispelled the spiritual darkness of the Middle Ages. Its widest field of usefulness, however, is afforded by conditions of the present day. Wherever religion has lost its reality, wherever ritual is more regarded than right living, wherever subscription to a creed is substituted for submission to Christ, wherever loud claims of orthodoxy are accompanied by conduct devoid of charity, wherever deeds of self-righteousness are obscuring the glory of the cross, there this epistle should be made to sound out its clarion call to a new dependence upon justifying grace, to a faith that is shown by works, to a walk that is by the Spirit, to a life inspired by love.

INTRODUCTION

Authorship and Aim

As to the authorship of this epistle there need be no doubt. It was written by Paul to defend the purity of the gospel against those who were insisting that Christians must observe the Mosaic law. Every paragraph is stamped with the personality of the great apostle. In him a powerful mind, a tender heart, and an indomitable will were united with the deepest spiritual insight; and this unusual combination of qualities in the author has given to the epistle its striking and characteristic features.

Never does Paul argue with more clearness, more incisiveness, more convincing power. Nowhere does he reveal more indignation, more scorn, more affection, more devotion to Christ, more consciousness of a divine call, more determination to accomplish a sacred task. The style is unmistakable. Its vigor, its irony, its pathos, its abruptness, its vehemence, its spiritual revelation, reveal Paul at the very height of his powers.

The special problem with which the epistle is concerned also argues for its authorship and its genuineness. By the end of the first century the relation of Gentile believers to Jewish ritual had ceased to agitate the church; but in the time of Paul it was a burning question, and its discussion held a central place in his career.

It was a matter of far greater difficulty and importance than one might suppose. The modern world has placed an unfortunate and an unnecessary gulf between Christian and Jew. No one today would dream that a Christian should be compelled to observe Jewish rites in order to attain the highest spiritual privileges and experiences. Yet this was exactly what many in the early church believed, and their contention was the occasion not only of this letter but of much of the writings and the anxieties and the labors of Paul. Judaism and Christianity are vitally related. Israel was the nation chosen of God to reveal to the world his being and nature, and his law and grace. Judaism is the flower of which Christianity is the fruit. Israel is the olive tree on to which Gentile Christians have been grafted as branches. The Old Testament prophets predicted the coming of Christ, the Messiah. The law of Moses, with its priesthood and altars and ceremonies, foreshadowed the redeeming work of Christ and the holiness expected of his followers.

However, Paul saw that, when the substance had come, the shadow could disappear; when Christ had fulfilled the law, he had become "the end of the law" to everyone who believed in him. Paul realized that even in Old Testament times men were saved by grace through faith in God as he had revealed himself; and Paul understood the great "mystery" that in Christ the law which separated Jew and Gentile had been done away, and that by faith in him Jews and Gentiles formed one body, the Christian church.

Many, however, did not share the vision of Paul. They insisted that even though Jesus were accepted as the Messiah, it was necessary for all who professed their faith in him to observe also with all strictness the ritual which Moses had established.

These legalists had much to support their contention. The inspired Scriptures showed the sanctity of the law. When Christ came he was careful, during all his ministry, to observe the requirements of the law. The apostles he ordained continued to frequent the Temple and to live and worship as other Jews. Even Paul, while proclaiming to Gentiles freedom from the law, continued to keep the Jewish feasts, to take upon himself Jewish vows, and to glory in his relation to the Jewish race.

It is no wonder that the legalists hated him, declared him to be a timeserver, denied his authority as an apostle, opposed his work, and pursued him to distant cities.

It fell to the lot of Paul not only to meet these enemies but to establish for all time the relation between law and grace, the doctrine of justification by faith, and the great fact that the Christian church is not a mere Jewish sect but a universal brotherhood, composed of all who trust in Christ and find in him the predicted Messiah, the fulfillment of all the types of ancient Scriptures and of all the hopes of the inspired prophets.

Paul was well prepared for his task. He was a Hebrew by birth, and belonged to the strictest of the Jewish sects, that of the Pharisees. He had studied the Mosaic law in Jerusalem as a pupil af Gamaliel, one of the leading Jewish teachers of the day. Yet Paul knew, also, the Gentile world. His birthplace was Tarsus, in consequence of which he had the high privileges of Roman citizenship. His early surroundings were those of Greek culture, for, after Athens and Alexandria, Tarsus was the most important university center of the age.

Such a man might well be selected as the one who was to teach the true relation between Judaism and Christianity. He had attained eminence as a student and teacher of the law. He passionately loved his own Jewish people, their history, their customs, their traditions and beliefs. He hated the church and sought to destroy all who accepted its doctrines. However, when he caught a vision of the glorified Christ, he saw that his atoning death was the fulfillment of all the Jewish sacrifices, and that his resurrection was a vindication of all his claims.

Henceforth, to Paul, Jewish ceremonies were matters of indifference. He observed them that he might give no offense to his Jewish friends, but he taught that they need not be kept by Gentile believers. He insisted further that to observe the law as a ground of salvation was in reality to turn from Christ and his atoning work.

On his first missionary journey Paul had made many converts among the Gentile inhabitants of Asia Minor, and had compelled none of them to observe the Mosaic ritual.

When he returned to Antioch, he was attacked by Christian converts from Judaism, who insisted that all believers must keep the whole ceremonial law. A great church council was called to meet in Jerusalem. There it was determined that the burden of the ceremonial law should not be bound upon Gentile believers. They were urged to avoid giving needless offense to their Jewish brethren, refraining from the use of food which had been sacrificed to idols and from blood; but they were completely emancipated from all observance of the Mosaic law.

However, the trouble was not ended. Not long after, Peter visited Antioch and, in rightful disregard of Jewish usages, sat at the same table with Gentile Christians. Then certain Jewish converts arrived from Jerusalem, who insisted that Jewish Christians would be defiled by contact with those who disregarded the ceremonial law. To their influence both Peter and Barnabas yielded. Paul, however, stood boldly by the doctrine of Christian liberty. He rebuked Peter before the whole church and completely discomfited the legalists from Jerusalem.

Nevertheless, the same difficulties arose wherever a Christian church was established. Judaizers appeared who attacked the doctrine of Paul, undermined his influence, and denied his apostolic authority. This was true in Corinth quite as much as in Antioch. In no place, however, was the attack so violent, so serious, and so successful as among the churches of Galatia. Here, as in the other churches, doctrinal difficulties had not arisen within the circle of the converts, but Judaizers had come from abroad and had invaded these churches, turning believers from the gospel of Christ, and insisting that they must observe the Mosaic law. The entire membership of these churches seems to have been affected. The situation demanded extreme measures. Therefore Paul wrote this epistle.

In no other letter does he set forth so clearly the perils of legalism, the glory of the cross, and the freedom from law which belong to the followers of Christ. This epistle is rightly called the "Magna Charta of Christian Liberty." It establishes the essential Christian truth of justification by faith, and by faith alone. No rites, no ceremonies, no form of worship or of words are necessary to salvation. All that is needed is faith in Christ. This faith, however, must be so real as to involve complete submission to his will, so vital as to manifest his virtues, so true as to follow his perfect law of love.

DESTINATION AND DATE

Which were the exact churches here addressed, it is difficult to decide. Did they belong to Galatia proper, or were they found within the larger Roman province known by that name? According to the former view, they were churches in the cities of Ancyra, Pessinus, and Tavium, which were established by Paul on his second missionary journey. According to the latter view, they were the churches in Antioch of Pisidia, in Iconium and Lystra and Derbe, organized by Paul on his first journey through Asia Minor.

The very name "Galatia" is of interest. Every schoolboy knows that "all Gaul" was "divided into three parts," but not every student of the Bible knows that certain Gallic tribes fought their way eastward through Europe, 278–277 B.C.; crossed the Hellespont; pillaged, plundered, and ravaged Asia Minor; and finally settled in the northern central plateau in a region which was designated Galatia, or "the country of the Gauls." The section to which the Galatians were finally confined, and which constituted Galatia proper, was a rough oval extending some two hundred miles east and west and some one hundred miles from north to south. It was inhabited in the time of Paul by a mixed population in which the descendants of the Gaulish tribes formed only a minority, while the larger number were of the ancient population, and to these were added many Greeks, Romans, and Jews. By the time of the apostle the region had passed under the power of Rome and formed part of a province which included within its southern borders the cities which Paul visited upon his first missionary journey.

In writing to the Galatians was Paul addressing churches of Galatia proper or churches of the Roman province, which included not merely Galatia but Paphlagonia and parts of Pontus, Phrygia, Lycaonia, and Pisidia? Was he addressing the churches of northern or southern Galatia?

In favor of the southern Galatia theory much can be said. In fact many modern commentators dismiss the traditional northern Galatia theory as no longer worthy of serious thought.

First of all, Paul frequently grouped the churches he addressed according to the Roman provinces in which they were located. Thus he wrote of the churches of Macedonia and of Achaia, and so possibly of Galatia.

Secondly, the cities of southern Galatia, such as Antioch and Lystra and Derbe, lay along the main routes of travel and were of far greater prominence than those of Galatia proper. It is probable that Paul addressed this important letter to the churches of these cities rather than to obscure churches of the north.

Thirdly, the establishment of the churches in southern Galatia is fully described in The Acts, whereas the visit of Paul to northern Galatia is mentioned by Luke only incidentally, if at all.

In the fourth place, the doctrinal question discussed by the apostle is said to have belonged to an earlier period of his ministry than that required by the northern Galatia theory.

To all this it has been replied:

1. Luke, the companion and biographer of Paul, certainly uses the term "region of Galatia" to denote not the Roman province but the northern part of the province (Acts 16:6; 18:23). Peter likewise seems to refer to northern Galatia, rather than to the Roman province, when he uses the term "Galatia" (I Peter 1:1).

2. Paul may have written many letters to the churches of southern Galatia. We have only a fraction of his correspondence, and the letters which have been preserved do not owe their place in the New Testament to the prominence of the parties addressed. Nor did Paul select the churches to which he wrote because of their size or importance, but because of their need and his concern for their welfare.

3. As to the establishment of churches in northern Galatia, Luke does refer to a visit there; and Paul's own description of his founding of the Galatian churches is almost conclusive in favor of the northern Galatia theory. He declares that his work in Galatia was not a part of his missionary program. It was due to an illness which turned him aside from his journey and detained him among the Galatians. To them, under such circumstances, he "preached the gospel." These circumstances seem quite unlike the description given by Luke of the first active, unresting, rapid itineration of southern Galatia, when Paul established churches in Antioch, Iconium, Lystra, and Derbe. Of this itinerary Luke has given a full description, and the more carefully it is read the less ground does it give for believing that this strenuous itineration could be attributed by Paul to a painful and repulsive "infirmity of the flesh." (Gal. 4:13-15.)

4. As to the statement that the doctrinal questions concerning the relation between law and gospel, between legalism and grace, had been settled earlier than the time of Paul's third missionary journey, and that this letter must therefore have been written at an earlier date, just the reverse is the contention of many careful students. In fact some assert that this epistle is so similar to the epistle to the Romans that it was quite probably written at nearly the same time.

Evidently there is much ground for divergent views. However, there does not appear to be any absolute reason for abandoning the traditional belief that the epistle was addressed to the churches of Galatia proper, in the northern portion of the province which bore that name.

According to this theory, the course of events in the life of Paul is as follows: On his first missionary journey he founds churches in Antioch of Pisidia, in Iconium, in Lystra, and in Derbe. On his second journey he passes through these cities, and then, when detained by an illness, preaches in old Galatia, and founds "the churches of Galatia," passing on thence to Troas and to Europe. On his third missionary journey, he returns to Galatia, visits the churches he has established, and then following the ancient royal road which traversed this region, he moves westward to Phrygia on his way to Ephesus. Either from Ephesus, or a few months later from Corinth, this letter is written, possibly in the year A.D. 57 or 58.

According to the southern Galatia theory, Paul's second visit to Galatia was identical with his return to Antioch, Iconium, Lystra, and Derbe on his second journey. He moves westward to Troas and Philippi and Corinth, and probably from the last of these cities writes this letter, which may be the earliest of the epistles of Paul extant.

Thus it is quite evident that the supposed location of these churches, whether in northern or southern Galatia, does affect one's view of the date of this epistle, and its place in the life of Paul. However, it does not affect the interpretation of the letter or its message for the present day. It is a question of real historical and biographical interest. It cannot be said to be of deep practical concern.

The substance of the letter is of supreme importance. Wherever the first readers of the letter may have resided, they received from Paul a document of priceless value. He was answering for them the question which concerned the very essence of Christianity. Was Christ sufficient for salvation? Must something be added to his atoning work? What must one do to be saved? Wherever written, by whomsoever first read, here is an epistle of vital concern to every human soul.

CONTENTS AND ANALYSIS

Every portion of the epistle is closely related to its one great theme; namely, Christian liberty. No other letter written by Paul is marked by a greater unity of purpose. The enemies of the apostle had discredited his gospel message and attempted to bind upon Christian believers the burden of the Mosaic law. With this in view they had denied his claims to be an apostle; while their own false teachings had resulted in serious irregularities of conduct. Therefore Paul found it necessary first to establish his apostolic authority, then to defend his doctrine, and finally to exhort to right living.

Thus the epistle falls into three sections of two chapters each. The first is personal; the second is doctrinal; the third is practical. The first concerns Paul's divine commission; the second, his doctrine of freedom from the law; the third, the life of believers. The first presents the apostle of liberty; the second, the doctrine of liberty; the third, the life of liberty. In the first the doctrine is stated; in the second the doctrine is defended; in the third the doctrine is applied.

The very salutation with which the epistle opens states Paul's apostolic authority as absolutely divine. (Ch. 1:1-5.) It is followed by a stern rebuke in which he expresses surprise at the fickleness of the Galatians; he charges the false teachers with heresy, and he repudiates insinuations against his own sincerity. (Vs. 6-10.)

Paul then asserts that the authority for his gospel has come from no human source, but directly from Jesus Christ. (Vs. 11-12.) This is the theme on which he enlarges during the remainder of the first two chapters. He proves the fact by a brief review of certain personal experiences which demonstrate his standing as an apostle.

1. He was an apostle before he had met the twelve apostles, whose recognized authority was alleged to disprove his own. He had been a leader among the Jews;

he had been a persecutor of the Christian church; but by a direct revelation from Christ he had been converted and appointed a messenger to the Gentiles. As to this call to service, he had consulted with no one. Three years later he did become acquainted with Peter and James. From them, however, he received no commission and asked no indorsement. He preached in Syria and Cilicia, and the churches of Judea thanked God for the task he was achieving. These churches recognized the divine call which his enemies were denying. (Vs. 13-24.)

2. When Paul met the apostles they recognized him as an equal. He had been preaching for fourteen years and went up to Jerusalem to consult about the gospel he was proclaiming. Here Peter, James, and John added nothing to his enlightenment or authority. They acknowledged him to be the apostle to the Gentiles, and, in recognition of his equality with themselves, they extended to him the right hand of fellowship. (Ch. 2:1-10.)

3. Paul had found it necessary to rebuke Peter, the reputed chief of the apostles. The occasion was this: Peter had visited Antioch, and, in accordance with the very principles Paul advocated, he had disregarded Jewish scruples and had eaten with Gentile believers. Then certain Judaizers arrived. They taught the very heresy the Galatians were accepting. They insisted that the Jewish ceremonial regulations must be observed. Under their influence Peter withdrew from his fellowship with Gentile believers, thus compromising his own sincerity and "the truth of the gospel." He was publicly rebuked by Paul, and the substance of the rebuke is reproduced at this point in the epistle.

The mention of this incident was a third proof of Paul's dignity and of his apostolic authority, and its recital gave Paul an opportunity of stating the great principle involved, the very theme of his epistle; namely, justification by faith in Christ and freedom from the bondage of the Mosaic law. (Ch. 2:11-21.)

Paul now turns to demonstrate his great theme. He brings forward a threefold argument and then makes a threefold appeal. (Chs. 3; 4.)

He argues first from the experience of the Galatians. They had received the Holy Spirit. This was the supreme and comprehensive Christian blessing. Had this come to them by their obedience to the law, or by their faith in Christ? They knew it was a free gift accepted by faith. Would they now abandon the principle of faith? Would they now seek by legal observances to perfect what had been begun by the Spirit?

Nor was their case exceptional. Their experience was the same as that of Abraham. He was justified by faith; and he was typical of all believers. By faith men become sons of Abraham; by faith they become heirs of the promises.

On the other hand, the law, with its requirement of perfect obedience, has the power only to curse and not to bless. For this very reason Christ came to redeem us from the curse, that by faith in him we might receive the promised blessing of the Spirit. (Ch. 3:1-14.)

In the second place, Paul argues from the character of the covenant made with Abraham. It was a gracious promise to be accepted by faith. It was made centuries before the law. It was not conditioned upon the law, nor could it be annulled by the law. Such a subsequent institution could not affect the promise made to Abraham and to his seed.

Yet the law had its purpose and its place. It was added to make men conscious of their sin. It was not given as a means of salvation, but to show the need of salvation. By its influence men might be led to accept the promise which could be received by faith in Christ. (Vs. 15-22.)

Paul argues, in the third place, from the state of immaturity of those living under the law. They were like children, minors, "infants," who had not attained to the age of "heirs," or of full-grown sons. The law was indeed their tutor, their pedagogue, their schoolmaster, sent to lead them to Christ. However, now that they had found Christ, they were no longer "under a tutor." They were full-grown sons; they formed the true seed of Abraham; they were "heirs according to promise."

Even though heirs, children, while still under age, need the tutelage of guardians, and have no part in their inheritance. Such was the condition of those under law. Now Christ has come. He has redeemed those under the law that they may be brought into the position of full-grown sons. As sons, God has sent forth his Spirit into their hearts, so that they call him Father and are no longer in a condition of immaturity and servitude, but are sons of God, enjoying their heritage, as heirs of the promises, by faith in Christ. (Chs. 3:23 to 4:7.)

To this threefold argument, Paul now adds a threefold appeal. First of all he appeals to the pride of the Galatians. In accepting the obligation of the law they felt that they had been admitted to a spiritual aristocracy among Christians. Paul assured them that on the contrary they were in effect turning back to their former paganism. To trust for salvation to the performance of rites and ceremonies is no better than to trust in idols. Ceremonialism may be but baptized heathenism. (Ch. 4:1-11.)

In the second place Paul appeals to their affection. He recalls the fervent reception they had given him when they first welcomed him as a messenger of the gospel. In spite of his physical infirmity, he had been received "as an angel of God." He deplores the alienation of their hearts which the false teachers have selfishly secured. He confesses his perplexity that his spiritual children should have turned against him and have doubted his message. (Vs. 12-20.)

In the third place he appeals to their intelligence. They who made their boast in the law should be able to see what the law itself teaches as to spiritual bondage and spiritual freedom. This is shadowed forth in the familiar story of Sarah and Hagar. Who received the blessing? Who became heir of the promises? Was it the son of the bondwoman or of the free? Was it the child "after the flesh" or the child of faith? So then those who trust in Christ are like children of the free. Instead of bondsmen to the law they are heirs of the liberty wherewith Christ has made them free. (Vs. 21-31.)

In the fifth and sixth chapters, Paul makes a practical application of his teaching. He shows that:

1. Christian liberty is imperiled by legalism. He urges his readers to maintain their freedom. He warns them that to accept circumcision will be to cut themselves off from Christ. It will bind them to keep the whole Mosaic law. It is either law or grace. They must choose between them. To the true Christian outward ceremonies are of little significance. "Faith working through love"—this is supreme. (Ch. 5:1-6.)

He cannot believe that they who started so well are to be turned from the Christian course. His own persecutions attest his loyalty to the cross. He believes that one who perverts the truth will not and ought not to escape punishment. (Vs. 7-12.)

2. Christian liberty is perverted as license. Its real complement is love, which is in essence the fulfillment of the whole moral law. This will be possible only as, by faith in Christ, one is energized by the Spirit. It is true that the Spirit will ever be opposed by "the flesh." But those who by the Spirit are set free from the bondage of law will by the Spirit be delivered also from the assaults of the flesh. The work of the flesh and of the Spirit are easily distinguished. Those that have been crucified with Christ and are living by his Spirit will keep the law, without either falling under the bondage of the law, or yielding to the license of the flesh. (Vs. 13-26.)

3. Christian liberty is perfected in love. This is illustrated by two examples. First, in relieving others of their

burdens of moral fault. By a humble, gentle restoration of a fallen brother, one may fulfill Christ's perfect law. (Ch. 6:1-5.)

As a second example, love should lead one to share his material goods with those who teach spiritual truth. Otherwise he will be mocking God. Sowing to the flesh or to the Spirit is preparing for an eternal harvest. Therefore one should do good to all men, assured that the time of reaping will come. (Vs. 6-10.)

The conclusion of the letter, written in bold characters by Paul's own hand, forms a compact summary of its entire contents:

1. In connection with chapters 5 and 6, Paul rebukes the Judaizers, as men who are not walking by the Spirit, but are insincere and sinister in their motives. (Ch. 6:11-13.)

2. In accordance with the teaching of chapters 3 and 4, Paul declares his whole ground of boasting to be the cross of Christ. (Vs. 14-16.)

3. As to his apostolic authority, established in chapters 1 and 2, no one should further question it. He bears, as brands of Christ's Lordship over him, the marks of bodily sufferings received in the service of his Master. (V. 17.)

The last line of the letter is in the form of an affectionate farewell. (V. 18.)

THE OUTLINE

V

I
THE INTRODUCTION
Gal. 1:1-10

A. THE SALUTATION   Ch. 1:1-5

1 Paul, an apostle (not from men, neither through man, but through Jesus Christ, and God the Father, who raised him from the dead), 2 and all the brethren that are with me, unto the churches of Galatia: 3 Grace to you and peace from God the Father, and our Lord Jesus Christ, 4 who gave himself for our sins, that he might deliver us out of this present evil world, according to the will of our God and Father: 5 to whom be the glory for ever and ever. Amen.

The salutations with which Paul opens his epistles are never mere literary formulas. They follow the forms used by writers of his day, but they are phrased with peculiar skill and are always pertinent to the particular letters in which they are found. Thus in addressing the Galatians the three usual parts of a salutation appear: first, the name of the writer; second, the description of the readers; and, third, the apostolic greeting. However, to these familiar features Paul adds phrases which are so unusual that the salutation forms a significant introduction to the epistle.

The name of the writer is arresting. It is that of Paul, the famous apostle, who stands supreme in his influence among all the followers of Christ. That he was the author of this letter there is not the slightest ground for doubt. Others of his writings have been questioned as to their genuineness. No one ventures to challenge this. Here the veil of intervening centuries drops away. We stand face-to-face with one who holds a foremost place in the history of the race. He is reciting chapters from his own

life, and the arguments thus enforced press upon the
hearts of his readers the reality of his teachings with a
power which none can resist.

Here one meets with Paul, and with Paul in his most
characteristic moods and utterances. Here appear the
subtlety and vigor of his intellect; here burst forth the
ardor and the passion of his soul; here are revealed his absolute devotion and submission to Christ; and here are
declared the essential elements of the faith which he proclaimed. With his own name Paul unites in this salutation a reference to his Christian companions, "all the
brethren that are with me." Possibly these were members
of some local church; more probably they were Paul's
companions in travel. For these obscure Christians it is
enough of glory that they enjoyed the confidence and
shared the labors of this great Christian leader who held
them in loving remembrance as he wrote these immortal
lines.

As to the exact churches here addressed, there is room
for decided difference of opinion. They were surely situ-
ated in the region now known as Asia Minor. They were
located near the center of that region. They were "the
churches of Galatia." However, whether they were located in the northern or the southern part of the Roman
province known by that name, it is difficult to affirm. If
located in northern Galatia, then they probably included
churches in the cities of Ancyra, Pessinus, and Tavium,
churches founded by the apostle on his second missionary
journey. If located in southern Galatia, then they were
the churches established during his first missionary journey
in Antioch of Pisidia, in Iconium, Lystra, and Derbe.

Sufficient facts are not forthcoming to justify a dog-
matic position in favor of either theory. It is evident that
the location of these churches would determine more exactly the time and place at which Paul wrote. Fortu-
nately, however, it does not affect the meaning or value of
his message. The great doctrines of justification by faith

and of Christian liberty, here set forth, apply to all churches in all places and times, and have a special import for the present day.

The greeting which Paul sends to these churches is summarized in the words "Grace . . . and peace." Possibly their familiarity may obscure their meaning. We expect them from the lips of Paul. He uses them continually as he begins his historic letters. They are not mere conventional phrases. They were current coin, but the great apostle stamped them with a new meaning, and in them embodies for his readers a prayer inclusive of the widest conceivable blessings. "Grace" was a salutation common among the Greeks. "Peace" was the salutation of the Hebrews. Paul so employed the terms as to give them for Christians a significance unique, tender, precious. "Grace" came not only to denote mercy shown toward the undeserving but to include all the blessings bestowed by God; while "peace" came to signify the sum of all the spiritual blessings enjoyed by man. "Grace" is the fountainhead of redeeming love, and "peace" the "river of life" that flows deep and calm through each believing soul. For ourselves and for others, we do well to offer this prayer which was so continually on the lips of the apostle, the prayer for "grace . . . and peace." Then, too, as one reads this letter, and notes its severe rebukes and stern warnings, it is well to remember that they come from the heart of one who longed to have his readers experience all the fullness of divine grace, all the blessedness of heavenly peace.

This salutation, however, does much more than designate the writer and the readers and express a prayerful greeting. It forms a real introduction to the epistle. To these three conventional elements of an opening salutation, such phrases are skillfully added as to present at once the essential themes of the letter. These are three. The first is Paul's apostolic authority; the second, the doctrine of justification by faith; the third, the life of

believers. To each of these three subjects two chapters
of the epistle are devoted, and to each of these subjects
definite reference is made in this salutation with which the
letter begins.

First of all, then, is the reference to Paul's authority as
an apostle. This evidently had been questioned by his
enemies at Galatia, and with a view to undermining belief
in his doctrines. So in the first syllables of his message he
affirms the genuineness of his apostleship. Therefore,
when the writer designates himself as "Paul, an apostle,"
he is using the term in its highest sense. Not merely is he
a "messenger" of Christ like Barnabas and James, the
brother of our Lord, who are called "apostles." Rather,
he claims to be on an equality with the Twelve. He is
not one of the Twelve but has the same ranking and cre-
dentials and mission as they.

He declares that he is an apostle, "not from men, neither through man." His authority is not from any human
source or through any human agency or channel. As to
the agency, it is "through Jesus Christ"; as to the source,
it is from "God the Father." The last phrase is to be
taken as referring to the peculiar and unique character
of the Sonship of Christ. God is here regarded as the
Father of Christ, and not, as elsewhere, the Father of
believers or the Father of all men.

The phrase is added, "Who raised him from the dead."
The resurrection of Christ was to Paul the proof of his
divine Sonship; it was also the completion of his exalta-
tion. Thus Paul regards his apostolic authority as conferred upon him not by the man Jesus but by the risen
and ascended Lord. His commission is in every respect
divine.

The risen Christ to whom Paul refers was also the crucified Christ, "who gave himself for our sins." Thus Paul
has in mind not only his own authority but the great
doctrine, the defense of which is to form the second division of the epistle. This is the doctrine of justification

by faith. It is significant, therefore, that in this introductory salutation he refers to the death and the resurrection of Christ "who was delivered up for our trespasses,
and was raised for our justification." All the "grace . . .
and peace" which Paul prays for the readers, in his greeting, come from "God the Father" as their source, but
from "our Lord Jesus Christ" as their channel. In him
God has revealed his "grace," through him God has bestowed his "peace." This has been made possible by the
redeeming love and self-sacrifice of Christ. He "gave himself for our sins." He laid down his life by his own free
act and will, and the occasion of his self-sacrifice was "our
sins." The object was to do away with our sins. "The
Son of man . . . came . . . to give his life a ransom for
many."

Where, then, is the need of the ceremonial upon which
the Galatians were basing their hopes of salvation? To
the death and resurrection of Christ nothing need be
added, nothing could be added. His redeeming work is
complete. In this single phrase Paul sums up the supreme
message of his epistle: "who gave himself for our sins."
Here we find the ground of our justification—not in works
of the law, not in ritual observances, but in Christ's atoning death.

However, justification must be followed by sanctifica-
tion. The ultimate purpose of God is to deliver us not
from the guilt of sin but from its power. This is the third
great theme of the epistle. Paul defends his apostolic
authority, but this is in order to establish the truth of his
doctrine, and he wishes to establish his doctrine, not as
an end in itself, but in order to secure holiness and purity
of life. Doctrine is never an end in itself; it is ever the
means to an end. Life is the ultimate goal of Paul's endeavor. Thus, the third portion of this epistle deals with
the life of victory over evil, the life of liberty and love,
which is enjoyed by those who put their trust in Christ.
He "gave himself for our sins, that he might deliver us

out of this present evil world."

More literally, "this present . . . world" is "this present . . . age." Paul here follows in his language the Jewish custom of dividing the history of the world into two great periods, the "age" preceding the future coming of the Messiah, and the "age" of the perfected Messianic reign. Wherever the gospel of Christ has gone, wherever the Lordship of Christ is recognized, there conditions and customs and life are transformed. Nevertheless, the age is still an "evil age." The hope of the world is for a better age—the age of glory which will dawn with the perfected Kingdom of Christ.

However, Christians are regarded as already delivered and redeemed. This deliverance is moral and spiritual. They are not taken out of the world, but are kept from the evil that is in the world. This deliverance was the very purpose and end of the work of Christ. He "gave himself for our sins, that he might deliver us out of this present evil world."

The origin of this deliverance, however, is found in the loving heart of God. It is "according to the will of our God and Father." Thus, as the apostolic authority of Paul had its source in the Father and its channel in the Son, so the redemption of believers is traced through the redeeming work of the Son back to "our God and Father."

No wonder that Paul breaks out in a spontaneous doxology, unique in that it closes a salutation: "To whom be the glory for ever and ever." The glory of God is his manifested excellence. This has been manifested in his Son. Measurably it may be shown in all the redeemed. To God, however, belongs and should be ascribed the praise now and forevermore.

B. THE REBUKE   Ch. 1:6-10

6 I marvel that ye are so quickly removing from him that called you in the grace of Christ unto a different gospel; 7

which is not another gospel: only there are some that
trouble you, and would pervert the gospel of Christ.   8 But
though we, or an angel from heaven, should preach unto
you any gospel other than that which we preached unto
you, let him be anathema.   9 As we have said before, so
say I now again, If any man preacheth unto you any gos-
pel other than that which ye received, let him be anathema.
10 For am I now seeking the favor of men, or of God? or
am I striving to please men? if I were still pleasing men,
I should not be a servant of Christ.

In opening his letters Paul usually follows his salutation with a thanksgiving. Here the thanksgiving is not
only conspicuously absent, but its place is filled with a
severe rebuke. It is even more asserting in that, while the
salutation closed with a doxology, in this rebuke Paul invokes a curse.

He wishes his readers to understand from the start
that he has serious matters to present. He is beginning no
mere academic discussion. The essence of the gospel is
at stake, and the glory of Christ and the salvation of immortal souls.

The rebuke is threefold. Paul rebukes the Galatians
for their fickleness, the false teachers for their heresy, and
his enemies for their charge of "timeserving." His language is not only vehement but solemn. He declares that
the Galatians are turning from God, that the teachers are
accursed of God, that he himself is loyal to God.

He begins by expressing his astonishment at the suddenness of the defection: "I marvel that ye are so quickly
removing from him that called you in the grace of Christ
unto a different gospel." He may mean that he is surprised that they are turning away from his teaching so
soon after their conversion or so soon after his second
visit to Galatia. Possibly, however, he may mean so
soon after the arrival of the false teachers. He is aston-
ished at the suddenness of the change, at the rapidity of
the movement, at the ease with which the Galatians had

yielded to the Judaizing doctrines. He is startled by their fickleness, appalled at their instability.

They have not taken, however, the decisive step. To prevent them from this he is writing. They "are . . . removing"; they are in the way of apostasy. However, Paul does not despair of them. Later in the letter he expresses his confidence in their personal loyalty and in the general soundness of their faith. Still, he sees the greatness of their peril. They "are . . . removing," or are proving themselves to be "deserters" or "turncoats" or "apostates." The case is intensely serious. They are not proving false merely to Paul, their teacher. They are not deserting a human cause or party. They are proving untrue to God. It was he "that called" them; and he called them to salvation "in the grace of Christ." The source of the call was the unmerited favor of God, which he revealed in Christ. In fact, the whole gospel which Paul had brought them as the messenger of God was a gospel of grace. Paul is distressed that the Galations are turning from God and his divine doctrine of grace to a doctrine of works which has been formulated by man.

They "are . . . removing . . . unto a different gospel," which is in reality no gospel at all. This is not exactly what Paul says, but it is in effect the meaning of his words. "Do I call it a gospel?" Paul seems to say. "But that might imply that it has a right to the name. This false teaching in reality is not another gospel. The only excuse for using the name in connection with the false teachers is the fact that their doctrine is a corruption of the gospel." This teaching, Paul insists, "is not another gospel: only there are some that trouble you, and would pervert the gospel of Christ."

In fact there is and can be but one gospel. This is the "good news" of salvation through Christ. It is not a system of human philosophy. It is not a religion invented by man. It is not even good advice in the form of a rule of living. It is "good news"; it is the announcement of a great redeeming work, the proclamation of a great reconciling act. It is the offer of peace and life through faith in Jesus Christ.

To pervert this "good news" into a system of rites or ceremonies or "works of the flesh" is to contradict God, and those guilty of such perversion deserve the condemnation and displeasure of God. "But though we," writes Paul, "or an angel from heaven, should preach unto you any gospel other than that which we preached unto you, let him be anathema."

The term "anathema" meant originally "devoted to God"; but as an animal, for instance, thus "set aside" as a sacrifice, is doomed to death, so the special sense of the word came to be "a curse," a "thing devoted to destruction." This is the sense of "anathema" throughout the New Testament; namely, "accursed." "Let him be anathema" must mean, therefore, "let him be accursed," or "let a curse be upon him," or "let the curse of God be upon him." It is thus the strongest possible form of condemnation.

Paul had warned his readers when with them of the peril of false teaching. He therefore repeats what he said then, "If any man preacheth unto you any gospel other than that which ye received, let him be anathema."

It should be noted that Paul speaks these solemn words not of men who are teaching infidelity or heathenism or atheism, but of those who professed to be preachers of the gospel of Christ. He pronounces "anathema" upon anyone who perverts that gospel.

The perversion which he had in mind is that which substitutes legalism for evangelism. To add anything to the atoning work of Christ, as a ground of salvation, is not merely to add to the gospel, it is to destroy the gospel. It is to proclaim a doctrine which is no gospel at all.

Law and grace constitute opposing systems, as do salvation by works and salvation by faith, circumcision and the cross, self and Christ. However, such is the pride of the human heart that men are ever attempting to substitute law for grace, and are ever attempting to secure salvation by ways of their own choosing.

There are those who put their real trust in rites and sacraments rather than in the living Christ whom these services should represent. Others have their real confidence in an orthodox creed. This is actually the idol which they worship. They believe in their acceptance with God because of their fierce defense of dogmas, even though they are grieving the Spirit of Christ to whom these dogmas relate.

Still others rest confidently upon their moral deeds, upon their culture, or upon their generous support of worthy causes. The entire church of the present day is in danger of legalism, of Galatianism, of substituting law for grace. Each believer needs to be called back again to that vital, humble, personal, transforming faith expressed by Paul in a subsequent chapter: "That life which I now live in the flesh I live in faith, the faith which is in the Son of God, who loved me, and gave himself up for me."

Paul has rebuked the Galatians for their fickleness and the false teachers for their heresy; he now rebukes all who may believe or may have circulated the charge that he is a timeserver. This form of slander had been given some seeming support by the conduct of the apostle. He had been careful to obey the law of Moses even after his conversion to Christianity. As an apostle he had kept Jewish feasts and performed Jewish vows and observed Jewish rites. Now, however, when teachers have come from Jerusalem insisting upon the necessity of observing the Mosaic institutions, Paul is pronouncing these men anathema. This surely looks like duplicity and insincerity.

The motive seemed to be quite obvious. Paul taught men what he thought they wished to be taught. To please the Jews he observed the law; to please the Galatians he proclaimed freedom from the law. The explanation appeared to be perfectly simple: Paul was seeking for popularity and human favor.

This is the charge he meets as he asks indignantly, "For

am I now seeking favor of men, or of God? or am I striving to please men?" To this charge there is the one sufficient answer; it is found in his Christian life and service: "If I were still pleasing men, I should not be a servant of Christ." His loyalty to Christ, his sufferings for the sake of Christ, were the evidences that he was seeking no human favor, but was conducting himself as a "bondservant," a "slave" of Christ.

Popularity with men cannot usually be secured along the line of devotion to the Master. This does not mean that loyal Christians cannot expect the love and admiration of countless friends who are true to the same Lord. Nor does it mean that men fail to recognize and to admire true Christian character. It does mean, however, that there are always those who are opposed to Christ and who refuse his gospel, who will feel enmity and will show hatred toward his followers.

Paul is absolutely certain that his course is not being determined by a desire for the praise of those who are disloyal to Christ and are seeking to corrupt his gospel. He is certain that as a servant of Christ he is doing the will of God.

This confidence explains the severity of the language he has just been employing. He can thus reprove the Galatians and can thus condemn the false teachers just because he is so sure that he is speaking for God as a servant of Christ.

Thus this reply to his accusers forms a fitting conclusion to Paul's surprising rebuke (vs. 6-10), and a true introduction to the defense of his apostolic authority which immediately follows (chs. 1:11 to 2:21).

II
PAUL'S APOSTOLIC AUTHORITY
Chs. 1:11 to 2:21

A. INDEPENDENT OF THE TWELVE APOSTLES
Ch. 1:11-24

11 For I make known to you, brethren, as touching the gospel which was preached by me, that it is not after man. 12 For neither did I receive it from man, nor was I taught it, but it came to me *through revelation of Jesus Christ.* 13 For ye have heard of my manner of life in time past in the Jews' religion, how that beyond measure I persecuted the church of God, and made havoc of it: 14 and I advanced in the Jews' religion beyond many of mine own age among my countrymen, being more exceedingly zealous for the traditions of my fathers. 15 But when it was the good pleasure of God, who separated me, even *from my mother's womb,* and called me through his grace, 16 to reveal his Son in me, that I might preach him among the Gentiles; straightway I conferred not with flesh and blood: 17 neither went I up to Jerusalem to them that were apostles before me: but I went away into Arabia; and again I returned unto Damascus.

18 Then after three years I went up to Jerusalem to visit Cephas, and tarried with him fifteen days. 19 But other of the apostles saw I none, save James the Lord's brother. 20 Now touching the things which I write unto you, behold, before God, I lie not. 21 Then I came into the regions of Syria and Cilicia. 22 And I was still unknown by face unto the churches of Judæa which were in Christ: 23 but they only heard say, He that once persecuted us now preacheth the faith of which he once made havoc; 24 and they glorified God in me.

After the introductory statements, the main body of the epistle consists of three divisions: First, the defense of Paul's apostolic authority (chs. 1; 2); second, a statement of Paul's doctrine, particularly justification by faith (chs. 3; 4); and, third, the application of his doctrine to life (chs. 5; 6). The first section is personal; the second is argumentative or polemical; the third is practical. The great theme of the epistle is Christian liberty. In the first section this theme is stated; in the second it is defended; in the third it is applied to life.

The argument for his apostolic authority is drawn wholly from Paul's biography. It is of special interest because in the English Bible it follows the last four chapters of Second Corinthians in which Paul makes a similar defense. Like that classic passage, these two chapters contain an explanation of Paul's life. They constitute an *apologia pro vita sua.*

There are three parts to the argument: First, Paul insists that he was an apostle before he met the other apostles (ch. 1:11-21). Second, when meeting them he was recognized as an equal by the apostles (ch. 2:1-10). And, third, he found it necessary to rebuke Peter who was the reputed chief of the apostles (ch. 2:11-21). It is evident that Paul's authority and the truth of his doctrine are inseparable. Thus, as he argues in these three paragraphs for his authority, in the first place he shows that his gospel was not learned in Jerusalem; in the second place, it was endorsed by the leading apostles; and in the third place, it was maintained against Peter, the most prominent apostle.

In establishing his position as an apostle, he contends that his gospel is not of human origin, but is absolutely divine and has come directly from God through Christ: "For I make known to you, brethren, as touching the gospel which was preached by me, that it is not after man. For neither did I receive it from man, nor was I taught it, but it came to me through revelation of Jesus Christ."

The first word of this paragraph relates Paul's contention as to the divine nature of his gospel, with the rebuke which immediately precedes. He was there pronouncing accursed anyone who should preach a different gospel; and he was there replying to his enemies who had accused him of duplicity and of "seeking the favor of men." Paul intimates that his vehement language is justified and that the seeking of human favor is inconceivable, "for . . . the gospel [which he preaches] . . . is not after man." It is not human in its character, its content, or its origin. Paul declares that he did not receive it "from man," nor was he "taught it" by man. He had not derived it from the apostles nor from any other human source. It came to him "through revelation of Jesus Christ." God was, therefore, the source of Paul's gospel message, but Christ was the agent by whom it was revealed to Paul. It came to him by means of a revelation which Jesus Christ had made. Paul does not explain the method which Christ employed. This method was not instantaneous nor should it be regarded as wholly miraculous, although it did have in it elements which were plainly supernatural. It should not be denied that before his conversion Paul had a rather definite knowledge of the great central truths of the gospel. These he refused to believe, but he had learned them from the lips of Stephen and the other martyrs in whose persecution and death Paul had a leading part. He had heard the facts relative to the life and the death and resurrection of Christ. He regarded the statement of these facts as foolish and blasphemous, but with their general character he was familiar.

Then came the marvelous experience of his conversion. He was on his way to Damascus when there was granted to him an appearance of the glorified Christ. It was this experience which was used to change his attitude toward the truth and to accept the great realities which formed the essence of his gospel message.

There was, however, a third phase to his experience. It

was while he meditated on his experience and the claims of Christ that the Spirit of God revealed more fully to him that gospel message which he went forth to proclaim in all the world. It was possibly such a comprehensive experience to which Paul refers when he declares of the gospel which he preached, "It came to me through revelation of Jesus Christ."

In order more fully to establish this contention as to the divine source of his gospel message, Paul argues first from his experiences before his conversion (vs. 13-14), and second from the earlier years of his apostolic preaching (vs. 15-24). As to those earlier experiences there had been nothing to incline him to the acceptance of Christianity, and no possible human source from which the gospel could have been derived. Paul had been a Jew, and one of the most strict in his adherence to the ancestral faith. He had not accepted Christianity because he had failed as a Hebrew. He had been foremost in his zeal for Judaism: "For ye have heard of my manner of life in time past in the Jews' religion, how that beyond measure I persecuted the church of God, and made havoc of it: and I advanced in the Jews' religion beyond many of mine own age among my countrymen, being more exceedingly zealous for the traditions of my fathers."

There had been nothing in his experience to explain or to prepare the way for his conversion. His great zeal had been shown in his bitter and cruel persecution of the church and in his endeavor to exterminate the followers of Christ. As a Jew he had surpassed the young men of his own age, both in his zeal for the law and in his defense of the traditions of his fathers.

The endeavor to account for the conversion of Paul on natural grounds has always been a failure. To suggest that he was greatly troubled by his conscience because of his cruelty to Christians, and that on his way to Damascus some physical malady precipitated an approaching crisis and made him imagine that he had caught a vision of

Christ whom he ever after claimed as his Lord, is quite contrary both to the history as given by Luke and to the statements which he here makes concerning himself.

Nothing could be more cruel or absurd than to style Paul an epileptic, and to endeavor thus to explain the transformation which occurred on his visit to Damascus. Paul was converted by a real appearance of Christ, and it was to this Christ that he owed his changed life and the content of his gospel. Paul himself realized that it was a supernatural experience, that his gospel came from a superhuman source, and that it was in its nature divine. He therefore declares that God had "separated" him, had set him apart, had marked him off from the rest of mankind, for his special task, even from the day of his birth. He further declares that it was by the grace of God that he had been called into the apostleship. This statement is quite in accordance with the phrase which so frequently opens his epistles; namely, "Paul, an apostle . . . through the will of God." He insists that, to prepare him for his ministry, God revealed "his Son in me." Following the outward revelation on the way to Damascus, there was this inner revelation to the heart of the apostle. The former would have had little meaning or power if it were not for the latter, and this inner revelation was in order that Paul might preach Christ among the heathen.

The burden of this message, the essence of this divine gospel, did not come, however, from Paul's inner consciousness. It was no dream, no philosophy of his own, nor did he secure it from the apostles in Jerusalem. "Straightway I conferred not with flesh and blood," writes the apostle: "neither went I up to Jerusalem to them that were apostles before me: but I went away into Arabia; and again I returned unto Damascus." Arabia was the region east and south of Palestine. Within its boundaries was the historic Mt. Sinai. In that region God had revealed himself to his people through Moses; and in that region, too, Elijah had received his revelation of the grace and power of God. It was to this region Paul went that he might have time for meditation and for prayer. There, in communion with his divine Master, he received that message which he henceforth was to proclaim to the Gentile world. For this special ministry he had been predestined; to it he had been graciously called by a supernatural vision; for it he had been prepared by the revelation of Christ which had burst upon his soul (v. 15).

From Arabia, Paul "returned unto Damascus." He did not go to Jerusalem as might have been expected. He returned to the place of his conversion, there to testify boldly for Christ, not to be taught the gospel, not to receive a commission from the Christian apostles. It is evident that Paul is insisting upon the divine origin and authority of his apostleship. It was "not from men, neither through man, but through Jesus Christ, and God the Father, who raised him from the dead."

It is not difficult to understand why Luke, in the ninth chapter of The Acts, makes no reference to this visit to Arabia which followed immediately upon the conversion of Paul. The purpose of Luke was not to give a narrative of the apostle's personal life. He was concerned specifically with the story of the Christian church; and he introduced personal matters only as they were vitally related to the one purpose which determined the selection of his literary material.

It is a little more difficult to find the agreement between the account, given by Luke, of the subsequent visit of Paul to Jerusalem and the account which Paul gives here in Galatians of that same experience. "Then after three years I went up to Jerusalem to visit Cephas, and tarried with him fifteen days. But other of the apostles saw I none, save James the Lord's brother." (Vs. 18-19.) According to the narrative of Luke, "Barnabas took him, and brought him to the apostles." According to the statement of Paul he saw only two of the apostles. There is no necessary contradiction here. The purpose of Paul in going to Jerusalem was to become acquainted with Peter. Not unnaturally, the apostles were afraid of the

powerful persecutor of the church until Barnabas introduced him to the apostolic fellowship. It would seem that
in addition to Peter, Paul met at this time only one other
person who was given the title of an "apostle."   James
was not one of the Twelve. But this man, "the Lord's
brother," held a place of great prominence in the Jerusalem church, and is here styled an apostle, together with
Peter.

The impression which Paul here intends to convey is
not at variance with the statements of Luke. He makes
it quite clear that his purpose in this visit to Jerusalem
was not to be taught the gospel or to receive apostolic
sanction. His introduction by Barnabas was not to secure
prestige for himself but to remove suspicion and fear from
the minds of the Jerusalem Christians. So important does
Paul regard this fact of his independence of human teachers, and so much is he troubled by the persistent false-
hoods of his enemies, that he makes a solemn appeal to
God in attestation of the truthfulness of his statements:
"Now touching the things which I write unto you, behold, before God, I lie not" (v. 20). The reality of the
divine source of his gospel warrants Paul in making so
serious an appeal.

He continues the argument from his personal history
by touching briefly upon experiences which filled with activity ten years of his early ministry. He insists, however,
that there was nothing in these experiences to indicate
any human source of his knowledge, or any authorization
by man of his recognized apostolic standing.   "Then I
came," he writes, "into the regions of Syria and Cilicia."
Syria is mentioned first because it was a province of far
greater importance than Cilicia, and further because the
ministry of Paul in Syria was of even greater significance
than that in Cilicia. It was in Antioch of Syria that Paul
had begun his notable ministry in companionship with
Barnabas. The latter had called the apostle from his
home in Cilicia to undertake the important tasks con-

nected with the founding in Antioch of the first Gentile church. It was from Antioch in Syria that Paul and Barnabas had set forth on their first historic missionary journey which brought them to Cyprus and then to the cities of southern Galatia.

During all this period of his labors Paul had not been in direct and personal relations with Judea and Jerusalem. He had not been receiving from those sources either guidance or instruction or authority. Judea was not the source of his knowledge of the gospel. "I was still unknown by face unto the churches of Judæa which were in Christ." It is a beautiful description of these churches to state that they were "in Christ." It may simply mean that they were Christian churches, but the implications are rather larger. It may indicate that Christ was the very sphere in which these Christians were living. His will, his Spirit, his service, formed the very elements in which they moved and worked. Of such churches Paul writes, "They only heard say, He that once persecuted us now preacheth the faith of which he once made havoc; and they glorified God in me." The joy of these Judean Christians is an essential part of Paul's argument. The Galatians were being led to distrust Paul. The false teachers in Galatia who claimed to have come with superior knowledge from Jerusalem were discrediting him. By way of contrast and to silence his enemies he declares that the "churces of Judæa which were in Christ" glorified God for the life and ministry of the apostle. This fact in addition should further establish in the minds of his Galatian readers his authority as an apostle.

B. RECOGNIZED BY THE APOSTLES
Ch. 2:1-10

*1 Then after the space of fourteen years I went up **again** to Jerusalem with Barnabas, taking Titus also with me. 2 And I went up by revelation; and I laid before them the*

*gospel which I preach among the Gentiles but privately be-
fore them who were of repute, lest by any means I should
be running, or had run, in vain. 3 But not even Titus who
was with me, being a Greek, was compelled to be circumcised: 4 and that because of the false brethren privily
brought in, who came in privily to spy out our liberty which
we have in Christ Jesus, that they might bring us into bondage: 5 to whom we gave place in the way of subjection,
no, not for an hour; that the truth of the gospel might continue with you. 6 But from those who were reputed to be
somewhat (whatsoever they were, it maketh no matter to
me: God accepteth not man's person)—they, I say, who
were of repute imparted nothing to me: 7 but contrari-
wise, when they saw that I had been intrusted with the gospel of the uncircumcision, even as Peter with* the gospel *of
the circumcision 8 (for he that wrought for Peter unto the
apostleship of the circumcision wrought for me also unto
the Gentiles); 9 and when they perceived the grace that
was given unto me, James and Cephas and John, they who
were reputed to be pillars, gave to me and Barnabas the
right hands of fellowship, that we should go unto the Gentiles, and they unto the circumcision; 10 only* they would
*that we should remember the poor; which very thing I was
also zealous to do.*

Paul is still continuing the story of his life. He is not
writing a biography, however, but is forging an argument.
Every detail of his personal history is intended to establish
his claims as an apostle of Christ. Nor is this his ultimate
purpose. His further and real aim is to convince his readers of the truth of his gospel message. In the preceding
chapter he had shown how his conversion and early
ministry had given no opportunity for the suspicion that
his gospel was of human origin, but all his activities had
intimated that his message and his mission came directly
from God.

He is now to show how one of the most important incidents in his life would support the same claims. This incident was that of the Council at Jerusalem which is

further described in the fifteenth chapter of The Acts. There are many today who question the identity of the incidents described in these two passages. Indeed there are those who take it for granted that the identification cannot be proved, who seem to feel that the case against such identification is absolutely closed. The probable explanation of the differences between the two accounts is that Luke had in mind his definite and continuous purpose of writing a chapter in church history, while Paul is concerned here with giving an account of his own personal and individual experiences. It would seem that the two accounts are easily reconciled if we understand that after Paul's arrival in Jerusalem there was first a private conference with the leaders of the church, which Paul describes here, and then the conference representing the entire church, which Luke describes.

Paul states that after the fourteen years of his early ministry, he "went up again to Jerusalem with Barnabas." These two evangelists, both of whom were often designated as apostles, had journeyed together through Asia Minor and had established there strong Christian churches. The membership of these churches was largely Gentile, and it was the very success of the mission of Paul that had raised the question among the Christian believers as to whether it would be necessary for converted Gentiles to observe the Mosaic law. Paul had declared for freedom from the law, but there were many in Jerusalem who held that in addition to having faith in Christ, the Jewish ritual must be carefully observed. Paul adds that when he went to Jerusalem he took "Titus also" with him. The selection of Titus as a companion was particularly significant. Titus was a Gentile. He had never submitted to Jewish rites, but had accepted Christ with no thought of keeping the Mosaic ritual. That he should accompany Paul to Jerusalem would only intensify and bring to a definite focus the question of the relation of Gentile believers to the law of Moses.

Paul declares that he "went up by revelation." There is no explanation of his exact meaning further than that he intends to signify that his going to Jerusalem was in accordance with the will of God which had been made plain to him. Whether this revelation was made to Paul alone or to the entire church at Antioch cannot be affirmed, but Paul felt sure that under divine guidance he was making this momentous journey to visit the mother church in Jerusalem.

Whether this "revelation" was made to Paul in person, or whether it was through the Spirit to the church, is not known. In either case, it gave to Paul the absolute assurance that it was the will of God for him to go to Jerusalem to attend the historic Council which determined for the church and for all time the very question which the false teachers had revived in Galatia. This was the question as to whether Christians needed to observe the Mosaic law. Therefore, in referring to this Council at Jerusalem, Paul not only further establishes his apostolic authority but also answers the very question which was troubling the churches of Galatia.

The difficulty which the Council was to settle had caused special trouble in the church at Antioch, at the close of Paul's first missionary journey. Certain Judaizing teachers had come from Jerusalem, insisting that all Christians in order to be saved must keep the law of Moses. In order to settle the controversy, Paul and Barnabas and other disciples were sent as a delegation to Jerusalem, where the matter was presented before a council representing the entire Christian church.

"I laid before them," writes the apostle, "the gospel which I preach among the Gentiles." The present tense of the verb, "preach," is significant. Paul is preaching the same gospel which he preached in Galatia. This gospel had received the sanction of the church in Jerusalem. Surely, therefore, Paul was no timeserver. He did not change his message to suit different occasions and hearers. If "a different gospel" had been preached to the Galatian churches, it was by false teachers and not by Paul. He knew only one gospel. To him a preacher of any other gospel was "anathema." He was justified in this position by his experiences at the Council at Jerusalem which he here narrates.

Before the public discussions, in which he took a prominent part, Paul first held private conferences with the recognized leaders of the church. He presented his case "privately before them who were of repute," probably to "the apostles and elders" of whom Luke writes in his account of the Council (Acts 15: 2, 4, 6).

Paul felt that the success of his whole ministry was at stake. He had no doubts as to the truth and accuracy of his gospel message. He feared, however, lest there might be some difference of view as to the necessity of keeping the Mosaic law. Such a difference might divide the church at Jerusalem, and so cause divisions in all the churches he had established. In fact, Paul felt that the very gospel was at stake and that all his work might be overthrown. He sought these preliminary private interviews, so he states, "lest by any means I should be running, or had run, in vain." He introduces this familiar figure of the foot race. If he could not convince the church leaders of the legitimacy of his gospel, he would be like a runner, who, in spite of all his efforts, was to be disqualified or was to lose the prize of victory.

In these important preliminary conferences the discussion centered upon the case of Titus. He was a friend and companion of Paul. As a Gentile, a Greek by birth, he had never observed the Mosaic law. He was a significant and crucial embodiment of the whole principle at stake. Some insisted that Titus should be "compelled to be circumcised." Those who so insisted are described by Paul as "the false brethren privily brought in, who came in privily to spy out our liberty which we have in Christ Jesus."

These "false brethren" may have been unconverted Jews, seeking to injure the Christian cause; but more probably they were Judaizing Christians who insinuated themselves into the councils of the church, secretly seeking some weak point of attack in order to discredit the preaching of Paul and particularly his doctrine of justification by faith and freedom from the burden of the Jewish law.

To these enemies of the gospel and of Christian liberty Paul absolutely refused to yield: "We gave place in the way of subjection, no, not for an hour." His determined opposition was due to the fact that he felt himself, in this case of Titus, fighting the battle for the whole church, and so, specifically, for the Galatian Christians. He contended for Titus, he declares to the Galatians, "that the truth of the gospel might continue with you."

Paul has been accused of inconsistency because in the case of Titus he refused to observe the Jewish rite which he had administered to his other friend and companion, Timothy (Acts 16:3). The principles involved were, however, quite different. In the case of Titus, Paul was refusing to admit the principle that observance of the Mosaic law was necessary to salvation. This was the doctrine of the Pharisaic legalists who opposed Paul in the Council at Jerusalem and who were represented by the false teachers troubling the Galatian churches.

In the case of Timothy, however, no such principle was at stake. Jewish Christians were not involved. Paul wished to avoid needlessly offending the unconverted Jews among whom he was to work. Paul made a concession to Jewish prejudices merely to avoid needless opposition. He permitted the rite as a matter of racial and social significance, and not as a ground of salvation. It was at most a practical compromise to make his companion more acceptable to the Jews. Furthermore, Titus was a pure Gentile, while Timothy was the son of a Jewess, and the question at issue involved the Christian liberty of Gentiles.

Paul gave by his personal practice similar grounds for the charge of inconsistency. He pleaded for freedom from the law, yet he himself observed the requirements of the law. (Acts 18:18; 20:16; 21:23-24.) He ever distinguished between ceremonial rites as a ground of salvation and as racial or national customs. The first are illustrated by the case of Titus; the second, by that of Timothy.

This distinction must be kept in mind throughout the epistle to the Galatians. Here Paul's objection to the law is to a system viewed as a proposed or imaginary substitute for the atoning work of Christ. The Council at Jerusalem was considering the way of salvation. Paul's attitude in the case of Titus was exactly that which he defends throughout the entire course of this epistle.

His reference to Titus has been quite pertinent to his whole argument. It has been introduced, however, in the form of a digression. He now returns to his narrative in relation to the apostles whom he met at Jerusalem. He shows how they set their seal upon his apostolic mission and message.

They are described as "those who were reputed to be somewhat." It is commonly supposed that Paul means to disparage those to whom he refers, and that his language is sarcastic. This is hardly the case. It would weaken his argument. The greater the actual worth and standing of these leaders, the more significant would be the fact that they extended to Paul "the right hands of fellowship." These leaders are probably the same as those "who were of repute" (v. 2), with whom Paul had first consulted "privately." They were almost certainly the Twelve.

Nevertheless, there may be something of irony in Paul's expression. The false teachers in Galatia had evidently made much of the alleged superior power and position of the "authorities," the "leaders," the "apostles" in Jerusalem, in order to disparage Paul. He now shows that he was recognized as an equal by these authorities, these persons of great reputation.

He adds by way of parenthesis, "Whatsoever they were, it maketh no matter to me: God accepteth not man's person." In speaking of what "they were" or "they once were" (v. 6, margin), Paul probably refers to their privileges and status as apostles who had known Christ during his earthly ministry and had been commissioned by him. Paul insists, however, that such supposed or real advantages made not the slightest difference to him and in no way affected the validity and independence of his mission. The reason was this: "God accepteth not man's person." He is not affected in his decisions or choice or approval by any outward appearance, or by human position or privilege. No matter what may have been granted to the primitive apostles, that would in no wise have concerned the truth of Paul's message or the authority of his apostleship, for the latter came directly from the Lord Jesus Christ.

As to these primitive apostles, however, Paul states that they "imparted nothing to me." They made no correction or addition to his gospel teaching. They recognized its soundness and its divine source. On what grounds then was it being questioned by the false teachers in Galatia?

Furthermore, instead of opposing him, they recognized that he had received a divine commission to preach the gospel among the Gentiles, just as Peter had to labor among the Jews. This conviction of theirs was based upon the fact that God, who had given such success to Peter in his sphere of ministry, had given like success to Paul as he preached the gospel to the Gentiles.

However, as to Paul's apostolic authority, most conclusive of all was the fact that James and Peter and John, who were recognized as "pillars," and supreme in their position in the church, gave to Paul "the right hands of fellowship" and commended him to his mission among the Gentiles.

There was, therefore, no question as to two different

doctrines. There was but one gospel. There was, however, a clear recognition of two spheres of labor. The Twelve accepted as their special province their Jewish fellow countrymen; Paul's particular sphere of ministry was to be among the Gentiles.

There was, however, one stipulation upon which the elder apostles insisted; namely, that Paul "should remember the poor," a requirement which he declared himself eager to fulfill.

"The poor" to whom reference is here made were undoubtedly the needy Christians in Jerusalem. Just why these Christians were in such special poverty one is left to conjecture. Some reasons can easily be supposed. Judea was frequently visited by famine. The Christians were the chief sufferers, owing to religious hatred and social ostracism, causes which, even in most favorable times, operated to make it difficult for them to secure a livelihood. Furthermore, they had attempted, in Jerusalem, a system of communism, which, despite its admirable features, seems to have shown more charity than wisdom, and may have contributed to the poverty of the church.

Whatever the causes, the condition was chronic and pitiful; and it is easy to see why the Twelve, and particularly why Paul himself, should be eager to secure aid from the wealthier and more favored Gentile churches. It was a course which human sympathy would prompt, but which would be encouraged by special regard for those of their own race and nation. Chiefly, however, and this was a weighty consideration with Paul, it would show to Jewish Christians the sincerity of Gentile converts, and would establish between these two elements of the church a bond of spiritual unity. It would be a safeguard against the very misunderstandings and alienations which were destroying the peace of the Galatian church, and were the occasion of this very epistle.

Therefore, on this point, as in all others, Paul was in perfect agreement with the Twelve, who unreservedly set their seal of recognition and approval upon his apostolic authority and doctrine and mission.

C. MANIFESTED IN REBUKING THE CHIEF OF THE APOSTLES Ch. 2:11-21

11 But when Cephas came to Antioch, I resisted him to the face, because he stood condemned. 12 For before that certain came from James, he ate with the Gentiles; but when they came, he drew back and separated himself, fearing them that were of the circumcision. 13 And the rest of the Jews dissembled likewise with him; insomuch that even Barnabas was carried away with their dissimulation. 14 But when I saw that they walked not uprightly according to the truth of the gospel, I said unto Cephas before them all, If thou, being a Jew, livest as do the Gentiles, and not as do the Jews, how compellest thou the Gentiles to live as do the Jews? 15 We being Jews by nature, and not sinners of the Gentiles, 16 yet knowing that a man is not justified by the works of the law but through faith in Jesus Christ, even we believed on Christ Jesus, that we might be justified by faith in Christ, and not by the works of the law: because by the works of the law shall no flesh be justified. 17 But if, while we sought to be justified in Christ, we ourselves also were found sinners, is Christ a minister of sin? God forbid. 18 For if I build up again those things which I destroyed, I prove myself a transgressor. 19 For I through the law died unto the law, that I might live unto God. 20 I have been crucified with Christ; and it is no longer I that live, but Christ liveth in me: and that life which I now live in the flesh I live in faith, the faith which is in the Son of God, who loved me, and gave himself up for me. 21 I do not make void the grace of God: for if righteousness is through the law, then Christ died for nought.

Paul is taking another step in his argument. His purpose is to prove his position as an apostle. With this in view he has related certain incidents in his personal career. First he has reviewed the story of his conversion and of his early ministry which were quite independent of the other apostles. (Ch. 1:11-24.)

Next he has shown how, at the Council at Jerusalem, he was recognized as an equal by the apostles. (Ch. 2:1-10.) He now recalls the occasion on which he found it necessary to rebuke Peter, the reputed chief of the apostles. Surely, then, his apostolic standing and authority must be at least as great as that of Peter, the recognized leader of the apostolic band. (Ch. 2:11-21.)

However, the purpose of Paul in proving his authority as an apostle was due in no sense to personal pique or pride. He was endeavoring thereby to establish the truth of his teaching. He believed that the gospel of Christ was at stake. Therefore his encounter with Peter is related, not only as the climax of his argument for his apostolic authority, but because it affords him an opportunity for stating the very essence of his doctrine. This doctrine he is to defend in the two chapters which follow. Thus the close of the personal portion of the epistle forms an admirable introduction to the doctrinal portion (chs. 3 and 4).

Moreover, the particular error to which Peter had given countenance was the very error which the false teachers were propagating among the churches at Galatia. Thus Paul's rebuke of Peter brings his readers to the very heart of his epistle. The exact time at which Peter "came to Antioch" (ch. 2:11), it is impossible to state. Most probably it was some years after the Council at Jerusalem to which Paul has just referred. At this Council it had been determined, for all time, that the observance of the Mosaic law was not a condition of salvation. However, the leaven of legalism was still at work in the Christian church. It soon took a more subtle and dangerous form. The Judaizers began to teach that legal observances placed believers on a higher plane than that of those who refused to be burdened by the ceremonial law. They attempted to establish among Christians an aristocracy of legalists.

They insisted that Gentiles who wished to be admitted to the inner circle of the followers of Christ must scrupulously obey the requirements of Moses. They attempted to establish a church within a church.

This was an insidious attempt to bind upon the necks of believers the intolerable burden of the law. Peter, while at Antioch, was led to countenance this endeavor. It was for this reason that Paul "resisted him to the face," because he had stultified himself. He had acted inconsistently; "he stood condemned" by his own conduct. "For before that certain came from James, he ate with the Gentiles; but when they came, he drew back and separated himself, fearing them that were of the circumcision." Those who "came from James" were evidently fanatical Jewish Christians, who were eager to bind upon all believers the Mosaic law. They had probably received letters of commendation from James, the head of the church in Jerusalem. He must not be suspected of any complicity in this legalist plot. While himself a strict observer of the law, he had defended, in the Council at Jerusalem, the cause of Christian liberty. He was ignorant of the use made of his commendation by the representatives of the legalizing faction at Jerusalem. However, Peter was swept away by their alleged authority, and by their specious arguments. He weakly yielded to what seemed to be the popular movement.

Before the arrival of these zealots, "he ate with the Gentiles"; that is, he associated freely with Gentile Christians, more specifically eating at the same table with them at the "love-feasts." Now "he drew back and separated himself, fearing them that were of the circumcision"; that is, the party of Jewish Christians who favored the observance of the Mosaic law. This course on the part of Peter was not due to conviction; it was occasioned by cowardice and was an act of insincerity and deceit. Yet it is not wholly surprising. It was in accordance with the weak strain in the character of the apostle. With the

strength and worth of that character all are familiar. His
love for Christ, his honesty, his loyalty, his impulsiveness,
his enthusiasm, have endeared him to every Christian
heart. However, none forget his lack of stability and his
timid sensitiveness to the opinions of others. Once before
his courage had failed—not his faith, but his courage—
and he had denied his Lord. Once again his courage has
failed and he is imperiling the gospel of Christ, denying
the full efficacy of his atoning death and seeming to countenance the substitution of works of law for the work of
the Spirit and the gifts of grace.

Affected by the example of Peter, "the rest of the Jews,"
that is, the Jewish converts at Antioch, "dissembled likewise with him." Most astonishing of all, "even Barnabas was carried away with their dissimulation." He who
had been the companion of Paul, who had seen the tri-
umph of the gospel among Gentile peoples; he who with
Paul had ever proclaimed the gospel of grace and freedom
from the law—even he became guilty of the same pitiful
hypocrisy.

The seriousness of the situation Paul was not slow to
realize. A stigma of uncleanness was being cast upon the
Gentile converts. The Jewish Christians were assuming
that the law could give some sanctity which faith in Christ
could not secure. To supplement the righteousness which
Christ offered was to declare it incomplete and ultimately
to supplant it. Paul "saw that they walked not uprightly
according to the truth of the gospel." He recognized that
they were really compromising the truth by casting the slur
of uncleanness upon those who had accepted the gospel
and were loyal to Christ.

Peter was the chief offender; Peter was most consciously
insincere; Peter above all the rest was guilty of deception.
Peter wielded the widest influence as the reputed chief of
the Twelve. Therefore Paul administered to him a severe
public rebuke in the presence of the entire church. "If
thou, being a Jew, livest as do the Gentiles, and not as do

the Jews, how compellest thou the Gentiles to live as
do the Jews?" (V. 14.)

It is a severe rebuke. Peter is charged with the most
flagrant inconsistency and with the most glaring insincerity. And he is guilty; he stands condemned. Years
before, on that housetop in Joppa, he had learned that
one should not regard as "unclean" that which God has
cleansed. He had laid aside his Jewish scruples and had
lived in free intercourse with Gentile believers. Now he
belies his own convictions. He acts in a way contrary to
his custom. He places a slur upon fellow Christians.
Merely to win favor with legalists from Jerusalem, he
lends the weight of his influence to compel Gentile believers to observe Jewish law. "Compel" was not too
strong a word to use; for if Peter countenanced even the
teaching that Jewish observances conferred a superior
sanctity or spiritual standing, it would be in effect a demand that all Gentile Christians should obey the Mosaic
law. For Peter to make such a demand was a betrayal of
Christian liberty; it was disloyalty to the gospel of Christ.
No wonder that Paul remonstrated in public with the
guilty apostle!

How far does the rebuke extend? Does it consist
merely in the charge that Peter was compelling Gentiles
"to live as do the Jews"? (v. 14). Or does the rebuke
continue through v. 16, or through v. 18, or through v. 21?
It is difficult to say. No one can affirm positively where
the rebuke ends and where the argument of the epistle
begins.

It is certain that when Paul publicly reproved Peter he
uttered more than the single sentence in reference to living as a Gentile. He must have proceeded to show the
inconsistency between Peter's conduct and Peter's beliefs.
Probably the remaining verses of the chapter are a brief
summary of Paul's public rebuke at Antioch; they form,
however, a superb introduction to his message to the
Galatians.

The point to be noted is that the position which Peter pretends to hold is exactly that of the false teachers who are troubling the Galatian churches. In rebuking Peter for his hypocrisy, Paul naturally states and advocates his gospel of grace. In relating the incident at Antioch, he finds occasion to give a concise outline of that gospel, and to set forth the doctrine of justification by faith, which in the following chapters he will proceed to defend.

This admirable summary of the gospel message (vs. 15-21) is both negative and positive. It shows, first, the insufficiency of the law and, second, the power of faith in Christ.

Even Jews, with all their superior privileges and advantages and attainments, have found it impossible to secure righteousness by the works of the law, but have been justified by faith in Christ. "We being Jews by nature, and not sinners of the Gentiles . . . ," writes Paul, "even we believed on Christ Jesus, that we might be justified by faith in Christ." There is probably something of irony in the words, when he speaks of "sinners of the Gentiles." Peter, and the party of legalists to whom he had yielded, had shown contempt for the Gentile converts with whom they had refused to eat. It was in accordance with the usual arrogant attitude of Jews toward men of other nations whom they regarded as "godless" and "unclean" and "sinners."

However, the Jews did form a holy nation and had inherited the covenants and promises of God. They had attained a certain sanctity in contrast with sinful Gentiles. Paul reasons from this fact, and he turns against the Judaizers their familiar language. He declares that in spite of all their privileges and regardless of their arrogant pretensions to superior holiness, even Jews, even men like Peter and Paul, had found that they could not be justified by works of the law, and had been compelled to turn to Christ for salvation. If, then, even Jews could not be justified by their attempt at keeping the law, why bind

the law upon Gentiles who had been saved, like Jewish
believers, by faith in Christ?

Paul's own conscience and the conscience of Peter, as
of all Jewish believers, had given the verdict that, judged
by the law, they were all sinners and under condemnation.
It was this conviction which had brought them to accept
Christ as their Savior.

This insufficiency of the law, which Paul and Peter had
recognized, and in view of which they had turned to Christ,
was in accordance with the statement of their Hebrew
Scriptures. The psalmist had declared that by the works
of the law "no man living" shall be justified (Ps. 143:2).
In all ages justification had been by grace and through
faith. Finally, in Christ the grace of God was fully revealed and all who accepted Christ and trusted Christ and
obeyed Christ were justified by faith and found acceptance
with God.

Since this was true, since the law could not justify and
justification had come by faith in Christ, what a reflec-
tion upon Christ to insist that the followers of Christ
lacked a righteousness which the law could supply! Or,
as Paul states the case, "If, while we sought to be justified in Christ, we ourselves also were found sinners, is
Christ a minister of sin?"

That is to say: If we Christians, who have regarded
ourselves as justified by faith in Christ, now resort to
legal methods, and Jewish rites and ceremonies, in order
to be justified, is that not confessing that we are sinners
and in need of being saved, and is not Christ then at fault
for our present sinful state? Can this be possible? "Is
Christ a minister of sin?"

Paul recoils from so monstrous a suggestion. "God forbid," he cries, using a phrase he commonly employed to
express horror and deprecation.

The real "sinner," the actual transgressor, is the one
who turns from Christ to the law, who tries to add to
justification by faith justification by works, who supplants

Christ by supplementing Christ, and who offers self-righteousness in place of the righteousness of Christ. "For if I build up again those things which I destroyed, I prove myself a transgressor." Paul here courteously puts himself in the place of Peter or his companions in error. He supposes himself guilty of taking so false a step. If he should go back to law as a means of salvation, then he would convict himself of sin in ever having renounced the law; or if it has been right to renounce the law, then it is wrong to return now to the law. In either case he would be not vaguely a "sinner" in condition, but a real "transgressor" in action.

By way of contrast to such an imaginary course, Paul now relates his actual experience, and over against the insufficiency of the law he pictures the all-sufficiency of Christ.

This insufficiency of the law as a means of salvation was twofold. Its moral standard was so high that in its light no man could be justified, and secondly, it had no power or principle that aided a man in meeting its demands. Christ held out a moral standard not one whit lower; but by his death he made atonement for sin, and by his resurrection and the gift of his Spirit he provided power for holy living.

Instead of finding in the law a way of salvation, by the very operation of the law Paul was led to abandon the law, that he might love and serve God. "For I through the law died unto the law, that I might live unto God." When Paul realized what the law really demanded, in all its deep meaning and implication, he discovered that he never could secure justification by his endeavor to keep the law. Rather the law passed on him a moral sentence of death. It revealed the reality and the depth of his sin; but it gave him no power to overcome sin. Therefore he turned from the law as a means of salvation, or of acceptance with God. He did so once for all, as truly as though he had died to the law. He could never return to it. He

could never again look to it, as the Galatians were looking
to it, as a ground of acceptance with God.

His relation to the law was broken as completely as
earthly relations are broken by death. Yet his purpose
was not that he might act in a way contrary to the law,
but that he might truly "live unto God," and attain that
experience of holiness he had sought for in vain under the
yoke of the law. (V. 19.)

Such, indeed, is the experience of every man who seri-
ously tries to save himself by keeping the moral law, by
personal uprightness, or by obedience to conscience. The
more truly he perceives the height and depth and length
and breadth of the law's demands, the more fully does he
understand that he can never meet those demands, and
the more eagerly does he turn from his own feeble efforts
to cast himself upon Christ, that in Christ he may find
pardon for past transgressions and power for holy living.

It was by identifying himself with Christ that Paul entered upon a new and truer life. When he surrendered his
will to Christ and came to trust Christ alone for his salvation, it was an experience in which he was so united
with Christ that in effect he partook of the death of Christ
and became one with the risen Christ: "I have been crucified with Christ; and it is no longer I that live, but Christ
liveth in me."

Crucifixion may picture the pain and anguish of soul
which accompanies death to self and a complete yielding
to the service of Christ. Here, however, it pictures the
absolute abandonment of Paul's former life of legal righteousness and confidence in the law. To all that world of
rites and ceremonies, as means of salvation, he was dead.
He died to them at the cross of Christ, for in that cross he
found the perfect sacrifice for sin, and by faith in the risen
Christ he found the source of true righteousness.

So truly was Paul surrendered to Christ that he could
say with all sincerity, "It is no longer I that live, but
Christ liveth in me."

That vital, spiritual union with Christ is a reality in which every believer should rejoice. The words, however, are not to be pressed with undue literalness. The person and personality of Paul were not destroyed. Christ and the believer are ever distinct. Two beings can never be merged into one. Personalities ever persist and are separate, no matter how much one may be influenced by another. Paul never ceased to think and act. His self-consciousness was not lost. His moral responsibility never was suspended.

There are those who have brought the doctrine of "the indwelling Christ" so far into the sphere of mysticism as to have bordered on fanaticism, and have taught the actual merging of the divine and human, so that only one personality can be said to exist, only one being to be conscious and active.

The corrective of such mystical teaching, the explanation of a true spiritual union, is given in the verse which follows. It is a union by faith. It is a continuance of the personality of Christ and the personality of the believer; and the relation between them is one of obedience, of trust, and of love. "That life which I now live in the flesh I live in faith, the faith which is in the Son of God, who loved me, and gave himself up for me." Paul is still living an actual life "in the flesh"; that is, in a mortal body. No matter how real his union with Christ may be, it does not end or suspend any of the natural functions and operations of mind or body. It is Paul, the individual, who still thinks and wills and chooses and hopes and fears, regardless of how much he may be influenced or strengthened by his divine Lord.

Faith is the link which unites the person of Paul with the person of his Lord. Faith becomes the channel through which Paul receives new power for living. Christ is the Object on which the faith of Paul rests. Some have supposed these words to mean that Paul lived "by the faith of the Son of God," as though it were the faith of Christ or Christ's own faith that saved Paul or gave him his new life. The words mean rather that Christ is the Object of Paul's faith.

It should be carefully noted that faith rests on a Person. We are not saved by believing in the death of Christ or in the work of Christ. We do believe these great realities and all they may import. Yet our faith, our saving, justifying, sanctifying faith, rests on a divine Person, "the Son of God."

Paul adds, "Who loved me, and gave himself up for me." This is the explanation of Paul's life, the sum of all his beliefs. In the death of Christ for him, Paul saw revealed the purpose and grace and love of God. All his efforts to save himself ceased. He accepted pardon and peace as free gifts, and in loving gratitude he went forth to serve the Christ who for his sake had died and risen again.

Paul declares that he does not, he cannot "make void the grace of God," as he indeed would be doing if he were attempting by works of the law to secure his acceptance with God. If men could have been justified by keeping the law, there would have been no necessity for the death of Christ. "For if righteousness is through the law, then Christ died for nought."

One who keeps the law as a ground of salvation virtually rejects the atoning death of Christ. The choice must be made between works and grace, between the law and Christ. The decision of Paul has been reached; it is final and changeless. What will be the choice of the churches of Galatia?

III
JUSTIFICATION BY FAITH
Chs. 3; 4

A. THE THREEFOLD ARGUMENT
Chs. 3:1 to 4:7

1. THE BLESSING ALREADY RECEIVED Ch. 3:1-14

1 O foolish Galatians, who did bewitch you, before whose eyes Jesus Christ was openly set forth crucified? 2 This only would I learn from you, Received ye the Spirit by the works of the law, or by the hearing of faith? 3 Are ye so foolish? having begun in the Spirit, are ye now perfected in the flesh? 4 Did ye suffer so many things in vain? if it be indeed in vain. 5 He therefore that supplieth to you the Spirit, and worketh miracles among you, doeth he it by the works of the law, or by the hearing of faith? 6 Even as Abraham believed God, and it was reckoned unto him for righteousness. 7 Know therefore that they that are of faith, the same are sons of Abraham. 8 And the scripture, foreseeing that God would justify the Gentiles by faith, preached the gospel beforehand unto Abraham, saying, In thee shall all the nations be blessed. 9 So then they that are of faith are blessed with the faithful Abraham. 10 For as many as are of the works of the law are under a curse: for it is written, Cursed is every one who continueth not in all things that are written in the book of the law, to do them. 11 Now that no man is justified by the law before God, is evident: for, The righteous shall live by faith; 12 and the law is not of faith; but, He that doeth them shall live in them. 13 Christ redeemed us from the curse of the law, having become a curse for us; for it is written, Cursed is every one that hangeth on a tree: 14 that upon the Gentiles might come the blessing of Abraham in Christ Jesus; that we might receive the promise of the Spirit through faith.

The third and fourth chapters of the epistle form its central doctrinal section. In the preceding chapters Paul has established his authority as an apostle, but in so doing he has prepared the way for the doctrinal discussion which now follows. He had argued from three incidents in his own life. The last of these was his public rebuke of Peter, who had been guilty of countenancing the very error into which the Galatian Christians were being led by false teachers from Jerusalem. His rebuke of Peter gave Paul an opportunity for stating clearly the doctrine of justification by faith which is the theme of the following chapters and is indeed the central truth of the Christian gospel.

It is this same doctrine which Paul sets forth in the five opening chapters of his epistle to the Romans. Here in Galatians, however, there is a different emphasis and a new element in his discussion. In Romans he is setting forth justification by faith, as the way of salvation, in opposition to the endeavor to secure acceptance with God by obedience to law, whether that law is the rule of conscience or the requirements of the Mosaic system. In writing to the Galatians, Paul is insisting that justification is by faith alone. The Galatians were being urged to add the observance of the Mosaic ritual to their faith in Christ as a ground of acceptance with God. The false teachers had not actually denied the work of Christ, nor had they urged the Galatians to abandon Christian truth. They taught, however, that Christians would attain to a fuller salvation and a higher sanctity and a superior place in the church if they would obey the requirements of Jewish law. Paul argues, however, that any attempt to thus supplement the work of Christ is in reality to supplant the work of Christ. He insists that there cannot be two ways of salvation, one through faith and the other through works.

As he closed the narrative of his rebuke of Peter, he did so by stating his own personal experience. He had once trusted in the law and attempted to save himself by obeying its precepts. His failure to keep the law, however, had driven him to seek some power outside himself. He had put his trust in Christ and had died to the law. He had become convinced that to ascribe saving power to the law was really to annul the death of Christ and to deny its redeeming grace.

This argument from the experience of the apostle forms the immediate introduction to his discussion of the doctrine of justification by faith.   This discussion consists of a threefold argument and a threefold appeal. The first argument is from experience, however; in this case it is not the experience of the apostle but of the Galatian Christians. He reasons from the blessing which they have received by faith.   This blessing consists of the gracious work which the Holy Spirit is doing for them. It is a blessing which has come through faith, and not by the observance of the law. Paul argues, therefore, that it is absurd for the Galatians now to turn away from Christ and to attempt by legal observance to seek for themselves an acceptance with God which faith in Christ had failed to secure.

His tone of address is severe.   "O foolish Galatians," cries the apostle, "who did bewitch you, before whose eyes Jesus Christ was openly set forth crucified?"   He regards them as senseless, as utterly bereft of reason, and as guilty of conduct which has no rational defense.   They must have been bewitched. Some magic spell must have been thrown over them. The word "bewitch" implies a reference to the familiar superstition of the "evil eye." Some malign influence has turned their gaze away from Christ. This influence is that of the false teachers.   They are, by some evil magic, diverting the eyes of their victims from the cross of Christ to the law of Moses. The Galatians, however, were without excuse, because Paul had plainly preached to them the efficacy of the cross, the full meaning of the death of Christ, and the complete salvation of those who put their trust in him. Before their eyes Jesus Christ had been "openly set forth crucified"; that is, he had been vividly depicted, graphically portrayed, as the

Savior who had died for the sins of the world, through
whose atoning death believers were granted acceptance
with God. Therefore the defection of these Galatians was
senseless and inexcusable.

It is not hard to imagine, however, the subtle reasoning
by which the Judaizing teachers had beguiled the Galatians. It was not difficult for them to picture the sanctity
and the divine origin and the long observance of the ancient law. Without much difficulty they could deceive
their victims and make them believe that, without abandoning Christ, they might attain merit by observing those
ceremonies which had been followed by the prophets and
heroes of old and by Christ and his apostles as well. Nor
is it hard for us to understand the fascination which rites
and ceremonies have for men of modern days, particularly
when these observances claim the sanction of antiquity and
of Christian tradition. It seems natural, also, even for
those who have accepted salvation through Christ, to seek
to add their own good works and deeds of merit to the
atoning work of Christ as a ground of acceptance with
God.

To those who are being thus misled, Paul continues his
rebuke. He now appeals to their former experience. "I
wish to ask you only one question," the apostle is saying in
effect. "This only would I learn from you, Received ye
the Spirit by the works of the law, or by the hearing of
faith?" The Galatian Christians, like other members of
the early church, had been granted miraculous spiritual
gifts, such as prophecy, the gift of tongues, the interpretation of tongues, the gift of healing. These gifts were the
signs and seals of their conversion and of the new life
which had been granted them. Paul asks whether these
gifts had been secured by the observance of the ceremonial
law or by believing in Christ. Had they received the Spirit
through doing what the law demanded or through believing the message which they had heard? Obviously these
gifts of the Spirit had not come by "works of the law" but
by "the hearing of faith."

"Are ye so foolish?" asks the apostle, "having begun in the Spirit, are ye now perfected in the flesh?" If these astonishing spiritual gifts have come to them along the pathway of faith, is it not folly to seek now for perfection along the line of ritual observance? It is to such observance that Paul refers by his phrase "in the flesh." While the law was in itself holy and righteous, while it was divine in its origin, yet was regarded as a means by which men could save themselves, it was then a mere human expedient, a matter external and formal, in contrast with the activity of the indwelling Spirit. How absurd then it was for these Galatians to seek for higher sanctity by actually descending from the plane of the Spirit to the level of the flesh, to turn from that which was divine to that which was human. They were not on the pathway of advancement, but in the way of failure and of loss.

If they were turning from Christ to the law, what advantage would remain from all that they had endured for the sake of Christ? "Did ye suffer so many things in vain?" asks the apostle. He refers to the persecutions and hardships which they had endured when they accepted the gospel. What advantage, then, would be theirs if they now abandoned the very principle of that gospel for which they had suffered so severely? Yet Paul adds, "If it be indeed in vain." He is not ready to abandon hope for his readers. He believes they may still see the folly of their course and may turn again to Christ in implicit faith.

With this in view he continues to argue from their personal experience. He turns, however, from the past to the present. Their former spiritual gifts had been received in simple faith. How about the present manifestations among them of spiritual power? "He therefore that supplieth to you the Spirit, and worketh miracles among you, doeth he it by the works of the law, or by the hearing of faith?" The word "supplieth" indicates a generous and gracious and rich bestowal. Paul generously intimates that the defection of the Galatians has only threatened or begun. God is still bestowing upon them abundantly the gifts of his Spirit. He is manifesting among them works of divine energy. Yet all this is being granted not on the ground of ritual observance, but on the ground of their believing the message which they have heard concerning Christ and his redeeming grace. Faith in Christ has been the source of their new life, the channel through which have come to them all their abundant spiritual blessings.

Nor is this principle of faith new or unique. It is the principle in accordance with which blessings have come to the people of God through all past ages, "even as Abraham believed God, and it was reckoned unto him for righteousness." The reference to Abraham is significant. To him the Jewish teachers would point with pride as being the father of their race, the source of their spiritual blessings. They would claim that by their obedience to the Mosaic law they would become heirs to the promises made to Abraham. To such supposed reasoning Paul makes a severe retort. He insists that all those who live by the principle of faith are the true children of Abraham and the heirs of the promised blessing: "Know therefore that they that are of faith, the same are sons of Abraham." Moreover, the inspired Scriptures testified to the fact that the blessings promised to Abraham were to be shared not only by Jewish believers but by Gentiles as well. Indeed, the promise to Abraham was in itself a gospel prediction, as it stated the "good news" of the blessings which those who believed would receive. As the apostle writes, "The scripture, foreseeing that God would justify the Gentiles by faith, preached the gospel beforehand unto Abraham, saying, In thee shall all the nations be blessed." It is accordingly those who live by faith who share the blessing promised to Abraham, "they that are of faith," who "are blessed with the faithful Abraham."

The folly of seeking for superior sanctity by legal observance is made still more evident as Paul now turns to another phase of his argument. Not only is it true that the blessings which his readers have experienced have been received through faith and not by obedience to the law, but furthermore it is true that while the law cannot bring blessing it can bring a curse. In fact, all who fail to keep its precepts and requirements perfectly are under condemnation. One must render an obedience which is complete and unfaltering, or else be subject to the curse which the law contains for all who fail to meet its perfect and exact requirements. "For as many as are of the works of the law are under a curse: for it is written, Cursed is every one who continueth not in all things that are written in the book of the law, to do them." Judged by such a standard, no man can be justified in the sight of God. Obedience not only must be free from all possible exceptions, but it must be continuous and unbroken.

Paul further argues that even the Old Testament Scriptures, which demand such explicit obedience and which pronounce so inevitable a curse, do not make any promise of justification to those who keep the law, but these very Scriptures set forth the principle of justification by faith. "Now that no man is justified by the law before God, is evident: for, The righteous shall live by faith; and the law is not of faith; but, He that doeth them shall live in them." The quotation from Hab. 2:4, "The righteous shall live by . . . faith," referred to a situation in which the people of God were in great peril, but in which deliverance was assured to the righteous who put their trust in God. Paul employs it here as a statement of a great principle in accordance with which those who trust in God are accepted as righteous in the sight of God. He contrasts it with the principle which is involved in the law; namely, a principle of works. In accordance with this principle Paul quotes from the law: "He that doeth them shall live in them." Compare Lev. 18:5.

When Paul declares that "Abraham believed God, and it was reckoned unto him for righteousness," or when he quotes the words of the prophet that "the righteous shall live by faith," Paul does not mean that faith is a substitute for righteousness. Nor does he mean that righteousness is merely imputed to those who believe. Faith is a living principle, and through it righteousness is not only imputed, it is imparted and experienced.

While the law cannot secure blessing, and while it pronounces a curse upon those who fail to keep its requirements, it is further true that this curse must rest upon all, for none have rendered perfect obedience to the demands of the law. From this curse, however, Christ has delivered those who have put their trust in him. He did so by himself assuming the place of penalty and suffering and shame. Believers had been like prisoners under condemnation, but Christ died for them. "Christ redeemed us from the curse of the law, having become a curse for us." This is the strongest possible statement of vicarious suffering. Christ took the place of the guilty. By his death he purchased for them redemption and pardon.

The very manner of his death involved the extreme of humiliation, disgrace, and shame. "For it is written, Cursed is every one that hangeth on a tree." This quotation from the Old Testament refers to the Hebrew custom, in accordance with which, after a criminal was put to death, his body was suspended from a tree or a post. Crucifixion was not a mode of capital punishment among the Israelites, but the disgrace of execution was intensified thus by hanging. The latter was regarded as witnessing in the presence of God that a just and sufficient penalty had been paid, and it was furthermore a testimony of God's abhorrence of sin. According to the requirement of the Jewish law, the body must be buried before nightfall, but while it remained exposed it was a public proclamation that sin had been punished. This reference to the ancient Jewish custom is made by Paul to indicate how truly Christ, in his death, endured the utmost ignominy and suffering for the sins of the world, even while he himself was sinless. He innocently bore the curse which was deserved by sinful men. His suffering, however, was endured in order that the blessings which had been promised to Abraham might come to all, of every race and nation, who would put their trust in Christ. The sum and the essence of all promised blessings were found in the gift of the Holy Spirit, a gift toward which all the promises pointed, a gift which could be received by faith alone. Thus, a third time within this paragraph (vs. 1-14) Paul reverts to the gift of the Spirit, a gift which his readers had experienced, and a gift which has come to all who have yielded themselves to Christ. If this supreme gift has been experienced through faith in Christ alone, it is surely foolish and senseless to seek for higher blessings by submission to rites and ceremonies imposed by men. None who have truly experienced the blessings of faith should submit themselves anew to the bondage of law.

2. THE CHARACTER OF THE COVENANT
WITH ABRAHAM Ch. 3:15-22

15 Brethren, I speak after the manner of men: Though it be but a man's covenant, yet when it hath been confirmed, no one maketh it void, or addeth thereto. 16 Now to Abraham were the promises spoken, and to his seed. He saith not, And to seeds, as of many; but as of one, And to thy seed, which is Christ. 17 Now this I say: A covenant confirmed beforehand by God, the law, which came four hundred and thirty years after, doth not disannul, so as to make the promise of none effect. 18 For if the inheritance is of the law, it is no more of promise: but God hath granted it to Abraham by promise. 19 What then is the law? It was added because of transgressions, till the seed should come to whom the promise hath been made; and it was ordained through angels by the hand of a mediator. 20 Now a mediator is not a mediator of one; but God is one. 21 Is the law then against the promises of God? God forbid: for if there had been a law given which could make alive, verily righteousness would have been of the law. 22 But the scripture shut up all things un-

der sin, that the promise by faith in Jesus Christ might be given to them that believe.

Paul is defending the doctrine of justification by faith. He has argued from the blessing already received—namely, the gift of the Holy Spirit—that acceptance with God is through faith and not on the ground of legal observance. While the law brought a curse for any disobedience to its demands, it had no power to bless. The principle of faith was illustrated from the case of Abraham, who "believed God, and it was reckoned unto him for righteousness." (Vs. 1-14.)

Paul now proceeds to show that this principle which operated in the case of Abraham is abiding and changeless. It was not affected by the subsequent giving of the Mosaic law. The promise to Abraham and his seed was without conditions. It was like a covenant which, when once made, could not be changed. It was unaffected by the law which was many years subsequent to it in point of time. The object of the law was not to secure justification but to reveal sin, and to turn men to Christ in whom the promise to Abraham was fulfilled. (Vs. 15-22.)

This step in the argument was necessary in view of the particular opponents whom Paul had in mind. The Jewish Christians who were troubling the Galatians were ready to admit that Abraham was justified by faith and that the Galatian Christians similarly through faith in Christ had been accepted of God. But they were insisting that the law of Moses, having been given subsequent to the promise to Abraham, was, therefore, binding upon the descendants of Abraham and upon all who expected to receive the promises which had been made to Abraham and his seed. These legalists granted that justification was by faith, but only in the case of those who had also observed the Mosaic law. They were insisting that, in addition to accepting the work of Christ, those who would be truly justified, surely those who would attain to the highest position as believers, must also obey the law which had been given through Moses.

It is this contention which Paul now meets. He shows the abiding validity of the promises made to Abraham and to those who by faith were his rightful heirs.

The tone of the apostle becomes less severe. He is now more intent than ever upon his argument, and is less concerned in rebuking his readers. "Brethren, I speak after the manner of men"; he is to make clear his argument by an illustration taken from the customs of daily life. "Though it be but a man's covenant, yet when it hath been confirmed, no one maketh it void, or addeth thereto." It is commonly recognized, the apostle is claiming, that an agreement between men when once signed and sealed cannot be annulled or altered by any third party, much less can the gracious promise which God made to Abraham be affected in its conditions and provisions by any subsequent requirement or demand.

The word "covenant," which Paul here employs, is somewhat difficult to translate, and has been the occasion of continuous debate. Possibly its strict meaning is that of a "disposition," or "a thing determined by expressed will." For this reason it has frequently been rendered by the term "testament," which is the common use in classical Greek, meaning a "testamentary disposition." This seems to be the best translation of the word in Heb. 9:16-17, where it is definitely connected with the death of Jesus. On the other hand, the word "covenant" was used in the Old Testament to describe an agreement between man and man. Neither of these exact meanings should be attached to the word as here employed, or as it occurs throughout the New Testament. The sense here is that of a gracious promise, or of a free undertaking and engagement to bless. It defines the disposition, the intention, the determined purpose of God. The argument of the apostle is that if a human agreement, when once ratified, cannot be annulled or overlaid by new stipulations, much less can the gracious promises given by God to Abraham and his spiritual descendants be made void or altered by the subsequent giving of the Mosaic law.

This argument, however, needs to be reenforced. Paul must show that the promise had not been fulfilled before the giving of the law, but that it found its true fulfillment in Christ and those who put their trust in him. If the promise had been fulfilled before the law was given, and if the blessings which Christians had received were not in fulfillment of the promise, then the restriction of the law might have come in to limit the promise, and Gentiles might have been compelled to accept the legal obligations which rested upon the Jews. For this reason Paul insists that God's gracious promise to Abraham and his descendants is realized only in and through Christ. "Now to Abraham were the promises spoken, and to his seed. He saith not, And to seeds, as of many; but as of one, And to thy seed, which is Christ."

When Paul here argues from a word used in the singular in contrast with a possible plural, he is accused of rabbinical quibbling. It should be noticed rather that there is tremendous force in his argument. He is insisting that the promise was not to all the descendants of Abraham, it was only to the line of true believers; and the promise ever found its goal in Christ, yet not in Christ alone, but in that great body of believers who are one with him. Paul is, therefore, presenting the great truth which becomes more and more clear through the course of the Old Testament, that the covenant blessings were to be realized in One who should sum up in himself all those to whom the promises had been made.

Since then the "covenant" was of such a character, since it was given long before the law, and since its fulfillment was found in One who appeared long subsequent to the giving of the law, it was evident that the law could by no means affect the covenant promise. "Now this I say," writes the apostle, as he applies the principle which he has already set forth: "A covenant confirmed beforehand by God, the law, which came four hundred and thirty years after, doth not disannul, so as to make the promise of none effect."

This statement of time, "four hundred and thirty years," is another ground on which Paul has been severely criticized. It is affirmed that he is here guilty of carelessness or of inaccuracy. As the sojourn of Israel in Egypt covered some four hundred years, it is evident that the time between Abraham and Moses must have been much longer. The difficulty must be recognized. However, it would hardly seem that Paul, with his careful training in the law, and his scrupulous exactness as a writer, was the man to make so glaring a mistake if he meant to measure, by four hundred and thirty years, the time between the first promise made to Abraham and the giving of the law at Sinai. One possible explanation is worthy of consideration. Reference is here made to "the promise," by which it may fairly be inferred that Paul has in mind the repetition to the patriarchs of the promise first made to Abraham. This covenant promise is said to have been "confirmed . . . by God," as indeed it was again and again. At the time that Jacob and his children were leaving Canaan for the long sojourn in Egypt, God confirmed his promise to the patriarch. The identical words are used which were first spoken to Abraham. (Gen. 12:2; 46:2-3.) It may not be unreasonable to suppose that it was from such a time, at which the promise was confirmed, that Paul is measuring the interval which extends to the giving of the law at Sinai.

It is, however, not necessary to remove this difficulty. The exact statement of the number of years does not determine the validity of Paul's argument. It is sufficient for his logic to insist that the covenant made so long before cannot possibly be affected by the subsequent giving of the law. The covenant was of the character of a gracious promise. To it no condition was affixed, save that of faith alone. The law proceeded on an entirely different principle. It was an agreement formed, involving the condition of implicit obedience.

If the promises made to Abraham are now to be conditioned upon obedience to the law, then they cease to be a gracious bestowal and designation of God. As a matter of fact, however, the promise made to Abraham was a gift of grace. There cannot, then, be two ways of salvation. It must be either by grace or by obedience to the law. The nature of the promise made to Abraham and fulfilled in Christ is, however, that of grace associated with no conditions of legal obedience; or, as the apostle declares, "If the inheritance is of the law, it is no more of promise: but God hath granted it to Abraham by promise" (v. 18).

To this argument as to the inability of the law to affect the promise made to Abraham and to be received on the ground of faith alone two objections are named. They may have been made by Paul's opponents, or they may have occurred to him as he reasoned with himself as to the relation between law and faith. The first objection is that the law is thus declared to be useless; it has no real purpose; it is futile (vs. 19-20). "What then is the law?"

Paul answers that the law was never intended to secure righteousness. It was rather intended to reveal sin. It showed men their need of justification. It convinced men of their inability to save themselves. It measured the depth and the guilt of human disobedience. It was divinely ordained to lead men to Christ. As Paul declares, "It was added because of transgressions, till the seed should come to whom the promise hath been made."

It is difficult to determine the exact meaning of the phrase "because of transgressions." Does it mean that the law was intended to keep men from the sins which it expressly prohibited? Or, on the other hand, does it mean, as Paul argues in his epistle to the Romans, that it was the design of the law to increase transgressions? Probably it signifies that the law was intended to make manifest the inward disposition or character of men as depraved and sinful. It was never designed to secure righteousness, but was ever intended to show the need of a Redeemer.

As Paul declares, the law "was added." It was no part of the original promise made to Abraham. That promise was independent of the law. Whatever the purpose of the latter, it could not invalidate the promise which was conditioned upon faith.

As further showing the inferior character of the law, Paul declares that "it was ordained through angels by the hand of a mediator." It might seem at first that this statement would glorify the law. It might remind one of the majestic scenes amid which the law was given, and of the divine sanctions under which it was enacted. On the contrary, the mention of "angels" and the reference to Moses intimate that the law was less gracious and permanent than the promise. The latter came directly from God, but the law was given through Moses. Nor did Moses himself receive the law directly from God. It was delivered to him on Mt. Sinai by the ministration of angels. Thus in the giving of the law, God is twice removed; but in giving the promise, God stands forth alone, independent, and sovereign. Hence the promise rests on a higher plane than the law.

" Now a mediator is not a mediator of one; but God is one." (V. 20.) It must be admitted that the meaning of this verse is not plain. It is estimated that it has received as many as two hundred and fifty different interpretations. It is reassuring, however, to find that among modern commentators there is practical unanimity. It is understood to contrast the law of Moses with the promise to Abraham. A "mediator" implies two parties at least. It indicates conditions which must be fulfilled, and a contract to which persons have agreed. This, indeed, was the nature of the law, but its conditions were never kept, and therefore the blessings which it promised were never received.

On the other hand, the promise depends for its fulfillment upon God by whom alone it was made; he gave it, and he will surely keep it, for all who trust in him. It was not related to the law, and its fulfillment was independent of the law's conditions and demands.

A second objection may therefore arise. (Vs. 21-22.) Is the law contrary to the promise? Does the one contradict the other? "Is the law then against the promises of God?" To this Paul solemnly objects. "God forbid," he replies. He will not entertain such a thought. The law and the gospel are not competitive or contradictory. The one is complementary to the other. Both have a part in the great economy of God.

Surely the law itself was not sufficient to secure salvation. Much less is it superior to the promise which is now embodied in the gospel. It demanded righteousness, but it had not power in itself to secure righteousness. It lacked any principle which could impart life. "If there had been a law given which could make alive, verily righteousness would have been of the law." Such, however, was not the case. Nevertheless, it had a part to play. It made men conscious of their sin and need. It, therefore, prepared the way for the fulfillment of the promise by making men conscious of their need of Christ. It was a strict, severe, yet necessary discipline to prepare men for the salvation which had been promised on the ground of faith. As recorded in the Scripture, it "shut up all things under sin, that the promise by faith in Jesus Christ might be given to them that believe."

By "all things" Paul means all mankind. The very purpose of the law was to bring a universal sense of condemnation. It shows men their sinfulness. It puts them in the prison house of remorse and despair until they long for the gracious deliverance which Christ offers and which he grants to those that put their trust in him. The legal system is therefore subordinate to the gospel, but it serves the ends of the gospel. It secures the very promise which the law in itself could never offer or provide.

The false teachers in Galatia were exalting the law as

superior to the gospel. They were insisting that only by
obedience to its precepts could men attain to the highest
position as followers of Christ. Paul shows by way of
contrast that the law is subordinate and inferior even
though it has a real part in securing the promises of grace.

There is a place for rites and ceremonies, if these are
used to make Christ and his power more real. There is
surely a place for conscience, and its commands must be
obeyed; but the highest function of conscience is to reveal
the need of a power outside of self and to lead a person to
Christ who can impart power for right living. Obedience
to conscience should not be regarded as a means to win
his favor; but gratitude to him, who saves us by his grace,
should inspire us to obey his holy will.

3. THE IMMATURITY UNDER THE LAW
Chs. 3:23 to 4:7

*23 But before faith came, we were kept in ward under
the law, shut up unto the faith which should afterwards be
revealed. 24 So that the law is become our tutor* to bring
us *unto Christ, that we might be justified by faith. 25 But
now that faith is come, we are no longer under a tutor.
26 For ye are all sons of God, through faith, in Christ
Jesus. 27 For as many of you as were baptized into Christ
did put on Christ. 28 There can be neither Jew nor Greek,
there can be neither bond nor free, there can be no male
and female; for ye all are one* man *in Christ Jesus. 29
And if ye are Christ's, then are ye Abraham's seed, heirs
according to promise.*

*1 But I say that so long as the heir is a child, he dif-
fereth nothing from a bondservant though he is lord of all;
2 but is under guardians and stewards until the day appointed of the father. 3 So we also, when we were children, were held in bondage under the rudiments of the
world: 4 but when the fulness of the time came, God sent
forth his Son, born of a woman, born under the law, 5 that
he might redeem them that were under the law, that we
might receive the adoption of sons. 6 And because ye are*

*sons, God sent forth the Spirit of his Son into our hearts,
crying, Abba, Father. 7 So that thou art no longer a bondservant, but a son; and if a son, then an heir through God.*

Ritualism is a sign of spiritual immaturity. The same
is true of the self-righteousness which trusts in its own good
works for acceptance with God, and the dogmatism which
seeks salvation by defending a creed.

Such, too, according to the apostle, was the condition of
those legalists, who, in order to secure a superior sanctity,
were adding to their Christian faith the observance of the
Mosaic law.

Paul insists that the law had kept the Jews in the state
of children under age, or at best had served as a tutor to
prepare them for the acceptance of Christ. On the other
hand, faith in Christ had brought them into the position
of full-grown sons, to whom belonged the privilege of free
access to the Father, into whose hearts God had sent the
Spirit of his Son, and who had indeed entered upon their
rightful heritage.

How foolish and senseless, then, for these Galatians to
seek for superior sanctity by submitting to the law! Instead of making an advance, this would be turning back to
a state of spiritual immaturity and bondage.

Paul is defending the doctrine of justification by faith.
He has shown that the legal system mediated through
Moses was merely parenthetic or preparatory. It could
not affect the covenant with Abraham and his seed, which
was of the nature of a gracious promise to be received by
faith alone. This promise was fulfilled in Christ and in
those who were united with him by faith. Christian believers were the true heirs of Abraham.

The law, however, had a function to perform. It revealed the need of righteousness and prepared for the acceptance of Christ. All who came under its influence were
made prisoners of sin that they might long for the gracious
deliverance which Christ freely offers to those who trust in
him.

"But before faith came," continues the apostle, "we were kept in ward under the law, shut up unto the faith which should afterwards be revealed." Thus the law is described as a stern jailer. Under it men were kept prisoners. Its restraints and limitations prepared them for the faith which was to be made manifest, and by which they were to attain the glorious liberty of the sons of God. "Before faith came," that is, before the coming of Christ, before the new dispensation, before faith in the Redeemer, the Jews "were kept in ward under the law." Paul does not mean that faith was a new principle. It had always been the instrument by which the people of God were justified. He does mean, however, to contrast the position of the Jews who had accepted the legal system with the freedom from the bondage of law enjoyed by the followers of Christ. The purpose of the law, however, was to lead to the acceptance of Christ and thus to fulfill the very end of the gospel. By it men were imprisoned, but they were "shut up unto the faith which should afterwards be revealed."

The intent of the law was, therefore, gracious and friendly. Paul is not content to describe the legal system merely by the picture of a jailer by whom men were kept in confinement until they should be delivered by Christ. The law introduced not only a period of imprisonment but one of preparation. Therefore Paul adopts another figure of speech: "So, that the law is become our tutor to bring us unto Christ, that we might be justified by faith." The law is subordinate to the gospel. It is inferior to the gospel, yet it makes men ready for the gospel. Its function is that of a "tutor."

Probably this is the best translation of the Greek word *"paidagogos,"* which Paul here employs. For this word there is no exact equivalent in English. It defines an office which does not exist in modern life. The "pedagogue," in the days of Paul, was a trusted servant, usually a slave, whose duty was not merely to lead his young master to school but in some measure to supervise his manners and morals. He was not qualified to instruct, nor was he given authority to control, but he was appointed to attend and to safeguard the child until his charge attained maturity and was no longer in need of guidance and discipline.

Such, according to Paul, was the place and function of the Mosaic law. It was a stern tutor intended for the guidance of the Jewish race. It regulated outward actions. It prescribed right conduct. It imposed certain checks upon evil until those under its guidance were ready for the spiritual freedom to be found in Christ.

When Paul declares that "the law is become our tutor to bring us unto Christ," he does not regard Christ as a schoolmaster. What he means is that the law has prepared us for faith in Christ. As Paul here intimates, Christ is the Object of our faith. The law prepares us to trust in him. We were brought to him "that we might be justified by faith." Thus the apostle adds, "But now that faith is come, we are no longer under a tutor" (v. 25).

When one trusts Christ for his salvation he ceases to be in the condition of spiritual immaturity which needs the care and discipline of the law. He now enjoys the liberty of a full-grown son, as the apostle adds, "For ye are all sons of God, through faith, in Christ Jesus." It may be noted that the Revised Version helpfully corrects the more familiar translation of the Authorized Version, which reads, "For ye are all the children of God by faith in Christ Jesus." It is well to observe the distinction between the term "children" and the term "sons." It is true that all Christians are the "children of God," as well as being "sons of God," but the two Greek words embody very different conceptions. "Children of God" denotes those who have been born again and who share the nature of God. The word "sons," which Paul here employs, denotes a legal status. It indicates the fact that Christians have certain rights and privileges, and that to these they are admitted through faith in Christ.

It is possible that the revisers have also improved the translation by the punctuation which they have introduced. By separating with a comma the phrases "through faith" and "in Christ Jesus," a new shade of meaning is revealed. The older translation is more simple and obvious, but the present rendering gives a deeper significance and specially prepares the reader for the statement which follows. If Paul here affirms that through the operation of faith we are all "sons of God . . . in Christ Jesus," he indicates that the sonship upon which we enter is enjoyed in view of that peculiar and intimate relationship with the Savior which is denoted by the phrase "in Christ Jesus."

Into such a relationship with him we are brought by baptism: "For as many of you as were baptized into Christ did put on Christ." Baptism here denotes a confession of faith. Without faith baptism would be an empty form. Unless Paul meant to denote an outward rite which expressed an inner yielding of the heart, he would have been guilty of the very error which he is attempting to correct in the Galatian believers. They were being taught that there was merit and saving efficacy in forms and in ceremonies; but the apostle was endeavoring to show them the sufficiency of faith. What he means, therefore, is to say that, when they accepted Christ, and when in baptism they expressed their devotion to him, they then "put on Christ." This last phrase denotes the taking upon oneself of the very virtues and excellencies of Christ. Faith is not merely an intellectual assent to certain doctrines. It is the going forth of the whole being toward a divine Person. It is the submission of the will to Christ. It implies devotion and obedience to Christ. It results here in a spiritual maturity which is manifested to the world by a likeness to the character of Christ.

There are some who feel that Paul is here connecting with the rite of baptism a figure of speech borrowed from Greek and Roman customs. When a Greek or a Roman youth passed from boyhood to manhood, the transition was marked by a change of costume. Instead of the *toga praetexta* he assumed the *toga virilis*. Formerly he had been under the rule of the family. He now took upon himself the responsibility of citizenship. It is possible that when Paul declared that in baptism the believer "put on Christ," he may have had such a custom in mind. There is no question, however, but that he here wished to indicate that one who was truly united to Christ by faith would manifest a likeness to Christ, and would enter upon a spiritual maturity quite in contrast with his previous state of tutelage and moral discipline under the dictation of the Mosaic law.

Spiritual maturity was, therefore, secured by faith in Christ. It was this which brought a man into a right relationship with God. It was this which made him in all reality a son of God. His standing, therefore, was dependent upon no human relationships or conditions. "There can be neither Jew nor Greek, there can be neither bond nor free, there can be no male and female; for ye all are one man in Christ Jesus." Paul does not mean that these differences have ceased to exist. He continually recognized them. He insisted on the duties of citizenship and the proprieties of sex. This verse should not be employed to indicate that for men and women there should be no distinction of functions and duties either in the family or in the church. Paul is here discussing a relationship to God, which is dependent wholly upon our faith in Christ and can be affected by no human distinctions or relations. He is arguing against the endeavor on the part of the Galatians to attain a higher standing by observance of the Mosaic law. He is insisting, however, that the very highest relationship, the full enjoyment of sonship, is dependent, not upon accidents of birth or of social standing, but upon faith in Christ alone. Those who are "in Christ" form one great brotherhood. They are all "one man," one son; and therefore all are heirs of the blessing promised to faith.

They are all "Abraham's seed." As Paul concludes, "If ye are Christ's, then are ye Abraham's seed, heirs according to promise." The force of the argument is that advantages of birth, of social position, or of human relationships, do not secure the promises made to Abraham. His distinction lay in the fact not that he was a Jew but that he was a man of faith, and therefore, whatever one might be by birth or social position, he would inherit the blessings promised to Abraham if only, like Abraham, he was possessed of faith. Believers are Abraham's true descendants and heirs of the blessings promised to him and to his seed. (Ch. 3:23-29.)

"But I say that so long as the heir is a child, he differeth nothing from a bondservant though he is lord of all." Paul is still illustrating the spiritual immaturity of those who lived under the Jewish law. They were like children under tutelage who were being prepared for faith in Christ. He now shows that they are no better than slaves in comparison with those who, through faith in Christ, have been granted the position of full-grown sons, enjoying their rightful heritage as the seed and heirs of Abraham.

In connection with this illustration various subtle questions have been asked. Is Paul referring to Gentiles as well as to Jews? Does he regard the father of the heir as living or dead? Is the illustration taken from the provisions of Greek or Roman or Galatian law?

As to the first question, it may be said that the same principles apply to Jews and Gentiles. While Paul is referring especially to the condition of Jews before they found Christ, Gentiles were also "under the law," and in Christ were given the full liberties of the "sons of God."

The second question need not be debated, and was probably not in the mind of Paul. He is fixing the thought of his readers upon the relations of the heir to his inheritance as determined not by the death of a father but by his attaining his legal majority.

As to the third question, the illustration does not correspond exactly to either Greek or Roman law, and it is improbable that the apostle concerned himself with the details of the obscure provincial code of Galatia.

Most of the answers to these questions, and the inferences based upon them, are more subtle than sound. The meaning of the apostle is perfectly clear. He wishes to picture the difference between the condition of a slave and that of an heir who has entered upon the enjoyment of his inheritance. His purpose is quite plain. He desires to guard the Galatians from the temptation to become entangled again in the bondage of Jewish law and to encourage them to enjoy the spiritual liberty which they have been granted through faith in Christ.

The message has its immediate application to believers in the present day. It raises the question as to whether, in their religious experience, they may be likened to slaves who stand in fear of God and are continually dreading the punishments of his broken law, or whether they stand in the relation of sons and enjoy loving fellowship with their Father.

"But I say," writes the apostle, indicating that he is to express his thought further in reference to the spiritual immaturity of those who are living under the tutelage of the law, "so long as the heir is a child," that is, a child under age, an infant at law, one who has not attained his maturity, "he differeth nothing from a bondservant," in respect, that is, to any possible control over his destined estate. He can no more enter upon its actual possession than could a slave in the household. In this regard he is in the exact condition of a bondservant, "though he is lord of all." He is an heir *de jure,* but not *de facto.* He is no more in the enjoyment of the promised possession than is a slave. "He is under guardians and stewards." During his period of subjection he is controlled and restrained by "guardians" who have charge of his person and trustees to whom is committed the care of his property. This subordinate and limited condition continues "until the day appointed of the father." This does not necessarily mean that the father is dead, or has made a speci-

fication in his will.   Paul is about to compare the limitation
of time imposed by human law and authority with the divine providence and purpose of God in whose hands all
destinies repose.   Here the phrase simply indicates the
time at which the supposed heir attains his destined inheritance.

"So we also," writes the apostle, having especially in
mind Jewish believers, "when we were children," that is,
while we were in a state of spiritual immaturity, as those
who were living under the tutelage of the law, "were held
in bondage under the rudiments of the world."   They were
kept, while under the law, in a process of preparatory
training.   The "rudiments of the world" refer to those elementary religious observances which, as interpreted by the
legalist, were merely outward and formal and material and
temporary, as contrasted with the abiding spiritual principle of faith in Christ.   These Jewish believers, while indeed having a great inheritance, were being instructed by
the legal system, as children might be trained by simple
symbols, by elementary object lessons adapted to imma-
ture minds.   This phrase, "the rudiments of the world," is
one about which there may properly be diversity of views,
but it can hardly be wrong to suppose that by it Paul is
making a reference to that whole system of legal rites and
observances which he has regarded as belonging to that period of discipline through which the Jews were brought in
preparation for their acceptance of Christ.

Of course there was another aspect of the law.   It was
divinely given, and for those high purposes to which Paul
had previously referred.   But he is wishing to show his
Galatian readers that their desire to adopt these Jewish
rites, as grounds of acceptance with God, would be merely
a proof and an indication that they lacked the maturity
which belonged to the true followers of Christ.   There are
some Christians today who fail to realize that trust in ritual
observances or in moral achievement or in doctrinal orthodoxy may indicate merely a relapse into second childhood

on the part of those who should know the freedom of full-grown sons.

It was the coming of Christ which brought the great crisis in the history of the people of God. His coming marked the period of release from the state of spiritual infancy and servitude, and of the entrance upon the promised possession. "When the fulness of the time came, God sent forth his Son." The preparation for the coming of Christ was mature and worldwide. It is needless to dwell upon the providences by which the Jewish race, and indeed the entire world, had been made ready for the advent of the Redeemer. Much might be said as to the conditions which favored his coming, such as the establishment of Roman law, the universal diffusion of Greek culture, and the wide dispersion of the Jews with their knowledge of the one true God and their belief in the coming of the Messiah. However, from what has preceded, Paul probably had in mind a different kind of preparation; namely, the universal sense of need, of moral helplessness, and of condemnation. It was in this respect that even the Jews, according to the apostle, had been "shut up . . . under sin," that by their very sense of guilt, which the law had produced, they might be ready for the acceptance of the Savior when he appeared.

"God sent forth his Son," forth from his throne on high, forth from the estate of his heavenly glory, "born of a woman," with all the limitations and weakness and helplessness of a human babe, "born under the law," subject to all its restrictions, requirements, and demands, yet born "that he might redeem them that were under the law." The purpose of the incarnation was redemption. The birth at Bethlehem looked forward to the cross of Calvary; but the ultimate purpose of redemption was "that we might receive the adoption of sons." Until Christ came, until redemption was accomplished, the state of spiritual immaturity continued; but when redemption had been achieved, then, through faith, believers might be received into the state, and might enjoy the privileges, of full-grown sons of God. Faith brings them into that blessed relationship. "And because ye are sons," writes the apostle, "God sent forth the Spirit of his Son into our hearts, crying, Abba, Father." The filial consciousness of the fatherhood of God was not possible until the Redeemer had appeared, and until, through faith in him, believers had entered upon the enjoyment of the promised inheritance.

Under the legal system represented by the Old Testament, the idea of divine sonship was veiled and indistinct. It is not altogether strange that men could not know God as their Father until the Son of God appeared. The words of our Savior are true in their strictest sense, "No one cometh unto the Father, but by me." He revealed the Father. He could say with all sincerity, "He that hath seen me hath seen the Father." He it was who, by his redeeming work, could bring men into a filial relationship with God. It is because we are sons of God that he has "sent forth the Spirit of his Son into our hearts."

The heart is especially the seat of the emotions, and it is because we are the sons of God, by faith in Christ, that his Spirit enables us to address the Father with accents of confidence and love. It is, indeed, the Spirit himself who cries within our hearts, "Abba, Father." The repetition of the Aramaic and of the Greek words for "father," the expression "Abba," our "Father," is a familiar form indicating loving and trustful entreaty.

The Holy Spirit is here well designated, "the Spirit of his Son." Since redemption has been accomplished, the Spirit of God has been so truly identified with Christ and his work that he is called the Spirit of Christ. The designation here assumed, "the Spirit of his Son," may rightfully be understood to indicate that the Holy Spirit proceeds from the Son as from the Father, that he is one with the Father and with the Son; but more particularly it intimates that it is his influence in the heart of the believer which awakens the consciousness of sonship, and which brings such a one into intimate filial relationship with God.

Thus in arguing for the great doctrine of justification by faith, as Paul began by reasoning from the blessings which faith had already brought to the Galatians, and as he found the chief and sum of these blessings to consist in the gift of the Holy Spirit, so here he attains the climax of his threefold argument by referring to this supreme blessedness which the Holy Spirit secures for the believer by assuring him of his divine sonship and thus bringing him into the enjoyment of his promised inheritance.

"So that thou art," concludes the apostle, "no longer a bondservant, but a son." How foolish, then, for the Galatians to fall back from their high position of spiritual privilege as sons of God to the standing of slaves under bondage to the law! Here Paul addresses each one of his readers as an individual, as he says, "Thou art no longer a bondservant, but a son; and if a son, then an heir through God." All that has been accomplished is "through God." It is all due to his grace, his mercy, and his love. He "sent forth . . . his Son"; he granted us the grace of adoption; he has brought each one of us into the position of a son who has entered upon the privileges of his inheritance. Redemption was in order to adoption, and because of adoption there has been the gift of the Holy Spirit. Even this gift, however, is but the "earnest of our inheritance"; for while, indeed, we now enjoy access to God and fellowship with him, there remains yet a fuller glory when the body itself has been "redeemed," when we shall dwell in the "Father's house," when we shall enjoy all that has been promised us as heirs of God and joint heirs of Jesus Christ. (Ch. 4:1-7.)

B. THE THREEFOLD APPEAL Ch. 4:8-31

1. AN APPEAL TO PRIDE Ch. 4:8-11

8 Howbeit at that time, not knowing God, ye were in bondage to them that by nature are no gods: 9 but now

*that ye have come to know God, or rather to be known by
God, how turn ye back again to the weak and beggarly
rudiments, whereunto ye desire to be in bondage over again?
10 Ye observe days, and months, and seasons, and years.
11 I am afraid of you, lest by any means I have bestowed
labor upon you in vain.*

Ritualism is baptized heathenism. Rites and ceremonies may be helpful. Like the requirements of the Jewish
law to which Paul has been referring, they may be of divine origin and gracious in their purpose. The sacraments
established by Christ may be channels of grace. However,
if these observances are practiced without faith in Christ,
they may be empty forms. If they are regarded as means
of obtaining divine favor, if they are offered to supplement
or to supplant the redeeming work of Christ, they are no
better than forms of pagan worship. To depend for salvation upon a ceremony which a man may perform is little better than trusting in an idol which a man may make.
Such at least seems to be the contention of Paul as he en-
deavors to restrain the Galatian Christians from adopting
the ritual of the Jews.

Paul has been defending the doctrine of justification by
faith. In his threefold argument he has shown that the
blessings promised to Abraham have been received through
faith in Christ. The Jewish law had been added long subsequent to the promise as a discipline preparatory to the
coming of Christ, and after redemption was accomplished,
believers in Christ enjoyed the liberty and the privileges of
sons of God.

Still further to establish his doctrine he now makes to
his readers a threefold appeal. He appeals first of all to
their pride. Most of them had been converted to Christianity from paganism. Their Christian faith had set them
free from the bondage of idol worship. Now they were being tempted to place themselves under the servitude of the
Jewish law. They were being assured that the observance
of this ancient ritual would make them more acceptable to

God and would enable them to occupy a higher place in the Christian church. Paul tells them that, on the other hand, to adopt these ancient rites which had long since served their purpose and were to these converted heathen mere meaningless forms would be in reality a relapse into pagan idolatry. The Judaizing teachers were priding themselves upon a superior sanctity. Paul here gives a severe thrust at their vanity by likening the Jewish ritual to the practices of heathenism.

He has prepared his readers for such a comparison and is now linking his appeal with his preceding argument, in which he had designated the Jewish observances as "rudiments of the world," and here again he describes them as "weak and beggarly rudiments." It must be insisted that Paul is not intending to reflect upon the sacred character of the Jewish law. He is intimating, however, that this legal system may be abused. It had its high function and purpose, but this had been served; and now to observe these ancient ceremonies as a ground of salvation was really to abandon the gospel of Christ.

He here addresses his readers not as Jewish but as Gentile converts. "Howbeit at that time, not knowing God, ye were in bondage to them that by nature are no gods." In the first word, "howbeit," he is intimating the pitiful contrast which he is about to suggest of a return to paganism from the liberty which his readers had secured in Christ. In their former state they had been ignorant of the one living and true God. They had been subject to cruel bondage as worshipers of gods which in reality did not exist. They had known the fear and the dread of idolaters, who worshiped deities which were not really such. Through Christ, however, they had "come to know God," with all the blessedness and joy which such a knowledge involves. However, Paul at once changes his figure of speech and insists that the experience of these heathen converts had been rather that of being "known by God." Paul will give none of the credit to man. He always insists that the ben-

efits of faith are matters not of human achievement but of
divine bestowal. Thus, the very knowledge of God was
due to his gracious revelation. They had been recognized
by God; they had been accepted by him as his sons.

Paul is distressed at the thought that they should now
turn from all the blessed privileges of sonship, back to a
state of religious slavery and bondage. "How turn ye back
again to the weak and beggarly rudiments, whereunto ye
desire to be in bondage over again?" He refers to the
Jewish rites as being feeble and poor. They once had a
divine power and value, but, since Christ has come with
his redeeming work, to adopt these ceremonies as a means
of salvation is to turn back to mere elementary religious
observances, to rudimentary notions and disciplines, which
for the Galatian Christians could fairly be compared to the
bondage under which they once had suffered as worshipers
of idol gods.

"Ye observe days, and months, and seasons, and years."
The reference is to the Jewish system of feasts and to the
Hebrew sacred calendar. Not only did it specify the observance of special days and annual festivals; it had also
its sacred month, its sacred year, and its sacred cycle of
years. In connection with this calendar a burdensome ritual had been brought into being. It would seem that the
defection of the Galatians had gone at least this far, that
they had undertaken to secure divine favor as Christians
by observing the Jewish cycle of sacred days. No wonder
that Paul is filled with consternation! Such a step can indicate little less than the speedy adoption of the whole Mosaic law. It will be abandoning the freedom which is in
Christ for a yoke of legal bondage. "I am afraid of you,
lest by any means I have bestowed labor upon you in
vain." He is really solicitous and anxious lest in effect
they should repudiate that Christian faith which they had
accepted in consequence of his faithful missionary labors
among them.

Nothing that Paul has here been teaching should be interpreted as condemning order and beauty in religious worship, or as denying the efficacy of Christian services and Sacraments. However, his words addressed to these Galatian Christians may be a warning to the followers of Christ lest the multiplication of forms and the reliance upon ceremonies may place a yoke of bondage on the hearts of believers and may rob them of the spiritual liberty which belongs to the sons of God.

2. AN APPEAL TO AFFECTION   Ch. 4:12-20

12 I beseech you, brethren, become as I am, for I also am become as ye are. Ye did me no wrong: 13 but ye know that because of an infirmity of the flesh I preached the gospel unto you the first time: 14 and that which was a temptation to you in my flesh ye despised not, nor rejected; but ye received me as an angel of God, even as Christ Jesus. 15 Where then is that gratulation of yourselves? for I bear you witness, that, if possible, ye would have plucked out your eyes and given them to me. 16 So then am I become your enemy, by telling you the truth? 17 They zealously seek you in no good way; nay, they desire to shut you out, that ye may seek them. 18 But it is good to be zealously sought in a good matter at all times, and not only when I am present with you. 19 My little children, of whom I am again in travail until Christ be formed in you— 20 but I could wish to be present with you now, and to change my tone; for I am perplexed about you.

The tone of the apostle becomes more tender. He appeals to the affection and sympathy of his Galatian converts and to the sacred memories of the past. The paragraph contains no statement of doctrine. It is wholly personal, but its sole purpose is to establish in the minds of his readers the truth of the gospel which false teachers are seeking to pervert.

Paul wishes that the Galatians might come to his point of view. He reminds them of the devotion they had shown

him when he first came to them with the good news concerning Christ. He warns them that the Judaizers are not
seeking their good, but are zealous only to further their
own mistaken cause. His desire is wholly for the Christian growth of the Galatians. His anxiety is for their spiritual welfare.

"I beseech you, brethren," he writes, sounding a note of
more tenderness than has yet been struck, "become as I
am, for I also am become as ye are." (V. 12.) He pleads
with them to take his position in the matter even as he has
taken theirs. The matter is that under discussion; namely,
that of the necessity of observing Jewish law. When he
first came among them as a messenger of Christ he re-
frained from observing his ancestral customs and his national traditions. He made no claim of superior sanctity,
but, though he was a Jew, he had been glad to enter into
fellowship with his Gentile converts. He now entreats
them to assume no superiority to him on the ground that
they are observing rites which for their sakes he himself
has been willing to abandon. He wishes them to regard
these rites as he does, to see that they are not necessary to
secure favor with God and that they are of no avail in ad-
vancing their spiritual life but rather are endangering their
Christian liberty and bringing them under a needless and
burdensome bondage. He implores them to exercise and
maintain the same freedom which he has shown and is still
defending. He has claimed no superiority on the ground
of Jewish ceremonial or legal observance. He has gladly
placed himself on a level with Gentile converts, regarding
himself as one with them in Christ Jesus.

He feels no ill will against them. "Ye did me no
wrong." He cherishes no grudge. He has been, and is,
deeply solicitous as to their spiritual state. He fears that
they are relapsing into a condition of legal servitude, yet he
harbors no resentment. Indeed, as he looks into the past,
it is only with a feeling of gratitude and of deep obligation to them because of the affection which they mani-

fested when first he brought to them the gospel message. "But ye know," he writes, "that because of an infirmity of the flesh I preached the gospel unto you the first time."

It is rather difficult to reconcile these words with the widely accepted theory that the churches to which Paul is writing were located in southern Galatia and were in reality the churches of Antioch in Pisidia, of Iconium and Lystra and Derbe. When on his first missionary journey Paul visited those cities and established there communities of Christians, he was apparently working with vigor and in accordance with a definite purpose. It is true that at Lystra he was stoned and left for dead; but it is improbable that he would describe this stoning by the phrase "an infirmity of the flesh"; and as we read the story as recorded by Luke there seems to be no place for such a bodily illness as is here defined. The statement of the occasion of his preaching to these churches seems quite as probably to indicate that his sojourn in Galatia was an unexpected experience, and, as is more commonly supposed, occurred during his second missionary journey, when passing westward through Galatia proper he was detained by a serious illness and, thus providentially detained, proclaimed the gospel message with such power that it resulted in the establishment of the churches to which he now writes.

Whichever view may be taken, there is no possible doubt that this first visit to the Galatians was attended by an illness, so severe and of so repulsive a character that the Galatians might readily have rejected the message because of the weakness and unattractiveness of the messenger. On the contrary, as Paul now writes, "That which was a temptation to you in my flesh ye despised not, nor rejected; but ye received me as an angel of God, even as Christ Jesus." They had shown to the ambassador of Christ as glad a reception and as ardent an affection as they could have shown to Christ himself. All this has now been changed. What has become of their former gladness, of their boasted blessedness, of their loud assertions of joy and gratitude?

"Where then is that gratulation of yourselves?" So grati-
fied were they then that the apostle had come, so thankful
were they to him for his service, so deeply did they appre-
ciate his message, that no sacrifice for his sake would have
been accounted too great. "For I bear you witness," he
writes, "that, if possible, ye would have plucked out your
eyes and given them to me." This statement has often
been interpreted to indicate that the malady from which
the apostle suffered was that of ophthalmia, or some other
painful affection of the eyes. This, of course, is quite possible, but the interpretation has been made popular possibly because of the translation of the verse in the Authorized Version which reads, "Ye would have plucked out
your own eyes." There is, however, no real reason for in-
serting the word "own," and Paul may simply have been
using a figure of speech to indicate that his hearers, in gratitude for his message, would have been willing to offer for
his relief that which was surpassingly precious. They
would even have sacrificed their sight as an expression of
their indebtedness to this messenger of Christ.

Why, then, this change in their attitude toward him? Is
it because he is still proclaiming that selfsame gospel which
formerly brought them such delight? "So then am I become your enemy, by telling you the truth?" He has not
changed; the gospel is not changed. Why, then, do they
treat him like an enemy? Why does he need to appeal for
sympathy and to plead with them to retain the truth which
he has proclaimed? He can himself make answer. The
change has been due to real enemies, to false teachers who
are seeking to corrupt the gospel. Unlike the apostle,
these teachers are purely selfish in motive. They have not
at heart the good of the Galatian Christians. They are indeed showing for them deep concern, but the motive which
moves them is not an eagerness to advance the interests of
these Galatian believers. "They zealously seek you in no
good way; nay, they desire to shut you out, that ye may
seek them." Their purpose and plan is to exclude the Ga-

latian Christians from their fellowship on the ground that they are on a lower spiritual level than these new teachers themselves, because they fail to observe the Mosaic ritual; the intention is, by thus excluding the Galatians, to compel them to adopt the ritual and to follow these false teachers with deferential zeal.

Paul does not deprecate such zealous attachment of disciples to teachers, nor such eagerness on the part of teachers to affect the belief and conduct of their followers. Such mutual affection between teachers and taught is ever highly desirable; only it must be in a good cause and with right motives. "It is good to be zealously sought in a good matter at all times, and," Paul adds, "not only when I am present with you." He wishes that the passionate devotion to him which the Galatians showed on his first visit might be continued when he is separated from them. It would fill his heart with joy to know that they still trust and love him. What distrsses him is the news that false messengers have so easily stolen away their hearts and turned them in bitterness against the apostle whose love for them is so true.

"My little children," writes Paul, using a phrase not found elsewhere in his writings, but quite common in the epistles of John—it is here employed to deepen the tenderness of his appeal—"I am again in travail until Christ be formed in you." The very pain and anguish of soul which the apostle endured in bringing the Galatian churches to birth he is again suffering because of their present failure and peril. He longs to have these Christians transformed into the likeness of Christ, but their development seems to be arrested. The very life of the churches is in peril. No wonder the apostle is in pain and distress! He would that he were with them. He wishes that he could speak to them even now while absent with a tone more tender: "I could wish to be present with you now, and to change my tone; for I am perplexed about you." It is true that he is here concerned with the purity of the gospel. He is, indeed, bent upon establishing the great doctrine of justi-

fication by faith. Yet aside from this deep and real concern, he is in anguish of soul because of the love and affection which he feels for his Galatian friends. Can it be
possible that they will resist an appeal so affectionate, so
loving, and so sincere as this? For his sake as well as their
own, will they not turn from all those influences which will
lead them astray, and will they not now seek for salvation
and for spiritual growth by a new abandonment of themselves to the will and service of Christ?

3. AN APPEAL TO INTELLIGENCE Ch. 4:21-31

*21 Tell me, ye that desire to be under the law, do ye not
hear the law? 22 For it is written, that Abraham had two
sons, one by the handmaid, and one by the freewoman.
23 Howbeit the son by the handmaid is born after the flesh;
but the son by the freewoman is born through promise. 24
Which things contain an allegory: for these women are
two covenants; one from mount Sinai, bearing children unto
bondage, which is Hagar. 25 Now this Hagar is mount
Sinai in Arabia and answereth to the Jerusalem that now is:
for she is in bondage with her children. 26 But the Jerusalem that is above is free, which is our mother. 27 For
it is written,*

Rejoice, thou barren that bearest not;

Break forth and cry, thou that travailest not:

*For more are the children of the desolate than of her
that hath the husband.*

*28 Now we, brethren, as Isaac was, are children of prom-
ise. 29 But as then he that was born after the flesh persecuted him that was born after the Spirit, so also it is now.
30 Howbeit what saith the scripture? Cast out the handmaid and her son: for the son of the handmaid shall not
inherit with the son of the freewoman. 31 Wherefore,
brethren, we are not children of a handmaid, but of the
freewoman.*

Paul has appealed to the pride and to the affection of his
readers; he now appeals to their intelligence. He addresses

in particular those who were inclined to yield to the Judaizing party. They claim to understand the Mosaic law and are willing to be bound by its precepts. Surely, then, they can see the force of an illustration drawn from the books of Moses. The case of Abraham furnishes an admirable parallel to that of the Galatian Christians who are hoping to be saved by adding legal observances to faith in Christ. Thus Abraham attempted to secure the promised blessing by the fleshly expedient of taking a slave girl in marriage in addition to Sarah his wife; but his real heir proved to be not the child of the slave girl but the son of the freewoman. The child of the slave was rejected; the child of the freewoman obtained the inheritance. So those who trust in Christ are the true sons of God, not those who seek his blessing by placing themselves under bondage to the law. The promised inheritance can be received by faith alone.

For no other portion of his writings has Paul been criticized so severely. He is accused of using a "rabbinical argument" to establish the doctrine of justification by faith. However, the allegorizing method of interpreting Scripture, brought into disrepute by the rabbis, and followed by many modern Christians who endeavor to "spiritualize" Bible history, differs essentially from the use of the illustration here introduced by the apostle. He does not use the Old Testament story as an argument to establish a doctrine but as a picture to make more plain a point already proved. The fault of rabbinical allegory and of modern "spiritualizing" lies in the endeavor to extract from historic narratives principles utterly foreign to the events recorded. In the case of Paul, however, he is recalling a story the very essence of which consists in the contrast between the false sonship of Ishmael with the true sonship of Isaac, the child of promise and of faith. How could he rebuke more severely the Judaizers who thus are put plainly in the place of Ishmaelites? How more impressively could he illustrate the contrast between the results of legal bondage and of Christian liberty?

"Tell me, ye that desire to be under the law, do ye not

hear the law?"   By hearing the law, Paul means under-
standing it, heeding it, appreciating its message.   Those
who desired to adopt it as a religious necessity should be
the first to understand its true import.   (V. 21.)   "For it is
written, that Abraham had two sons, one by the handmaid,
and one by the freewoman.   Howbeit the son by the handmaid is born after the flesh; but the son by the freewoman
is born through promise."   This is not a quotation from
the Old Testament, but it is a brief summary of the story,
the principle of which Paul wishes to apply.   The two sons
of Abraham are, of course, Ishmael, the son of Hagar, and
Isaac, the son of Sarah.   The former "is born after the
flesh"; that is, according to the ordinary course of nature.
"The son by the freewoman is born through promise."
The birth was according to the promise of God, through
the faith which Abraham reposed in that promise, and by
a miraculous intervention which brought the promise to
pass.

"Which things contain an allegory."   No doubt is raised
as to the historical truth of the story by regarding it as an
allegory.   It is given a higher value as it is shown to embody a spiritual reality and to typify the abiding relation
between those who are under spiritual bondage and those
who enjoy Christian liberty.

"These women are two covenants."   That is to say, Hagar and Sarah typically represent the two covenants, of
law and of grace.   "One from mount Sinai, bearing children unto bondage, which is Hagar."   The first of these
covenants is from Mt. Sinai.   It was there at the foot of
the quaking mountain that the people of God bound themselves to observe the requirements of the law.   All those
who accepted such bondage are properly pictured as children of Hagar.   Thus Hagar rightly stands for Mt. Sinai in
Arabia, the country to which the literal descendants of Hagar belong.   Hagar, therefore, rightly represents "the Jerusalem that now is," those who are still subject to the law,
the existing Judaism, the advocates of which are troubling
the Galatian church.   This present Jerusalem "is in bond-

age with her children." On the contrary, "the Jerusalem that is above is free, which is our mother." The heavenly Jerusalem, the spiritual city of which all Christians are members, is not under bondage of the law, and all its citizens should claim and maintain the liberty secured by Christ. By a quotation from Isaiah, Paul pictures the joyful spirit and the rapid growth of the heavenly Jerusalem, the true church of God.

"Rejoice, thou barren that bearest not;
  Break forth and cry, thou that travailest not:
  For more are the children of the desolate than of her that
    hath the husband."

Isaiah, the great prophet of the exile, was describing the restoration of literal Jerusalem, the enlargement of her borders, and the coming greatness of the rebuilt city. The prophet is employing the figure of a wife long deserted but now accepted again by her husband and fruitful in children. Of this predicted blessedness the experience of Sarah had been a type. In contrast with Hagar she had long been childless, but ultimately rejoiced in the birth of a son through whom all the families of the world were to be blessed. The ultimate fulfillment of type and prophecy, as Paul indicates, is to be found in the joy and blessing and fruitfulness of the Christian church. Its blessing may seem long delayed, but all those who are citizens of the Jerusalem that is above will rejoice in the increasing prosperity and in the ultimate glory of this heavenly city. As Paul applies the allegory, he plainly declares, "Now we, brethren, as Isaac was, are children of promise." We who by faith belong to Christ are those who are destined to receive the inheritance. For the time being we may be afflicted, persecuted, despised, but the ultimate blessing is assured. The Galatian Christians who were true to the gospel of grace might be scorned and excluded by those who were zealous for the Jewish law and wished to bring them under its bondage, but nothing should persuade them to forfeit the liberty which was theirs by right as followers of Christ. "But as then he that was born after the flesh persecuted him that was born after the Spirit, so also it is now." Ishmael's persecution of Isaac as recorded in the ancient story consisted in his insolent derision, but it was indicative of the attitude and conduct of an elder son who was jealous of the heir and felt enmity toward him. It was typical of the Judaizing teachers who wished to take from the Galatians their birthright of spiritual liberty.

"Howbeit what saith the scripture? Cast out the handmaid and her son: for the son of the handmaid shall not inherit with the son of the freewoman." The expulsion of Ishmael from the patriarchal home brings a stern rebuke to those who seek to secure a place in the church both for the bondage of the law and for the freedom that is in Christ. Paul here indicates clearly that there can be no place for legalism in the Christian church. He indicates that the true children of Abraham are those who inherit the promises by faith. "Wherefore, brethren, we are not children of a handmaid, but of the freewoman." He will now urge his readers so to live. He will enjoin them to maintain their liberties. The closing portion of the epistle will exhort them to hold fast to their freedom. Its keynote is sounded in its opening verse: "For freedom did Christ set us free: stand fast therefore, and be not entangled again in a yoke of bondage."

The peril of the Galatians confronts the church of the present day. There are many insidious influences which would incline the followers of Christ to accept some form of legal bondage and to forfeit the freedom of faith. Christians should be on their guard lest they seek for salvation by any other means than that of faith in Christ alone. As grounds of acceptance with God, no human expedients or efforts are needed or can avail. We must be careful not to put our observance of ceremonial rites, our defense of orthodox beliefs, our propriety of conduct, or our deeds of charity, in place of the redeeming work of Christ.

IV
CHRISTIAN LIBERTY
Chs. 5:1 to 6:10

A. IMPERILED BY LEGALISM Ch. 5:1-12

1 For freedom did Christ set us free: stand fast there-
fore, and be not entangled again in a yoke of bondage.
2 Behold, I Paul say unto you, that, if ye receive cir-
cumcision, Christ will profit you nothing. 3 Yea, I testify
again to every man that receiveth circumcision, that he is
a debtor to do the whole law. 4 Ye are severed from
Christ, ye who would be justified by the law; ye are fallen
away from grace. 5 For we through the Spirit by faith
wait for the hope of righteousness. 6 For in Christ Jesus
neither circumcision availeth anything, nor uncircumcision;
but faith working through love. 7 Ye were running well;
who hindered you that ye should not obey the truth? 8
This persuasion came not of him that calleth you. 9 A
little leaven leaveneth the whole lump. 10 I have confi-
dence to you-ward in the Lord, that ye will be none other-
wise minded: but he that troubleth you shall bear his
judgment, whosoever he be. 11 But I, brethren, if I still
preach circumcision, why am I still persecuted? then hath
the stumblingblock of the cross been done away. 12 I
would that they that unsettle you would even go beyond
circumcision.

Paul here passes to the practical portion of his epistle.
He presses home the results of his argument. He reaches
the climax of his appeal. The first two chapters were concerned with Paul's apostolic authority; the third and fourth,
with the doctrine of justification by faith; these last deal
with the maintenance of Christian liberty. The first two
chapters were personal; the second two were polemical;
these last are practical. In the first two the doctrine of

Christian liberty was stated; in the second it was defended; in the third it is applied. Or, as some have described these three great divisions of the epistle, the first presents "the apostle of liberty"; the second, "the doctrine of liberty"; and the third, "the life of liberty."

It is true that many prefer a slightly different analysis and insist that the opening section of chapter 5 (vs. 1-12) belongs to the preceding division of the epistle (chs. 3; 4). There can be no doubt that the relation of these verses to those which precede is vital. Paul has established his doctrine of justification and has shown that the believer is free from the bondage of the law. He proceeds now to show how this great truth is related to life and action.

In this regard he makes three great affirmations: First, Christian liberty is imperiled by legalism (ch. 5:1-12); second, it is perverted as license (vs. 13-26); third, it is perfected in love (ch. 6:1-10).

So closely is the first of these sections united with the preceding argument that some regard its opening clause as a part of the preceding sentence, and even render the sentence thus: "Since we are children of the freewoman, Christ having made us gloriously free, stand fast and do not again be hampered with the yoke of slavery."

However, it may be sufficient to regard this first phrase as the summary of the argument which precedes and the basis for the practical exhortations which follow. "For freedom did Christ set us free: stand fast therefore, and be not entangled again in a yoke of bondage."

Freedom is the rightful heritage of the followers of Christ. He secured this precious prize at infinite cost. They are the true children of "the freewoman." They are the rightful heirs of liberty. To set them free from the law, Christ died for them. He came to "redeem them that were under the law," that they "might receive the adoption of sons." Into their heart God has sent "the Spirit of his Son," crying, "Abba, Father." So they are no longer bondservants but sons, and if sons, then heirs through God.

Shall these Galatians forfeit all these rights? Shall they renounce their liberty? Shall they bind upon themselves the fetters of the law?

It is to prevent such a tragedy that Paul sounds forth his appeal: "Stand fast therefore, and be not entangled again in a yoke of bondage." The freedom of which the apostle writes is freedom from the law of Moses, not as a guide to life or a rule of conduct but as a ground of acceptance with God or as a means of salvation. Paul had taught that justification is by faith in Christ, apart from the law. The Galatians had accepted salvation as a gift of God. They had been saved by grace and not by works.

It is against the loss of this spiritual freedom that Paul warns his readers. They had formerly been in bondage to false gods (ch. 4:8). They were enslaved by heathen worship and customs. To place upon their necks now the yoke of the Jewish law would be to make them relapse into a state of servitude. They would be "entangled again in a yoke of bondage."

The statement may sound severe, but ritualism is really a form of heathenism. To attempt to save oneself by ceremonies is merely a form of paganism. Nor is the self-righteous man more wise, who rejects the salvation offered by Christ and seeks acceptance with God on the ground of his own good works. Even Christians, who like the Galatians have accepted the gospel of free grace, are tempted to lose their spiritual liberty, and under seductive influences to bind upon themselves a yoke of servitude to some ritual or moral code or way of life devised by man.

Paul sees the peril and therefore proceeds, first, to warn the Galatians of their danger (ch. 5:2-6), and, second, to condemn the false teachers to whom the danger was due (vs. 7-12).

The peril was far greater than might be supposed. The Galatians had not been asked to surrender their Christian faith, but to add to the work of Christ their own keeping of the law as a second ground of their acceptance with

God. Paul insists that there cannot be two grounds of salvation, two methods of justification, two ways of life. To accept the one involves the rejection of the other.

"Behold, I Paul say unto you, that, if ye receive circumcision, Christ will profit you nothing." The tone is stern and imperative. Paul has ceased to argue. He speaks with the full weight of apostolic authority: "Behold, I Paul say unto you." Yet this introductory phrase intimates more than authority. It indicates that the pronouncement about to be made is of supreme importance. The climax has been reached. The ultimate word is to be uttered. Listen to the sum of the whole matter: "If ye receive circumcision, Christ will profit you nothing."

There can be no compromise, no divided allegiance, no combination of contradictory methods. The choice must be made. It is either law or grace, either faith or works, either self-righteousness or the righteousness provided by God, either circumcision or Christ.

If justification is sought through circumcision, it cannot at the same time be received through Christ. If it is the ground of confidence and hope, then Christ is no longer the sole and sufficient Savior. "Christ will profit you nothing" in the securing of righteousness, in the obtaining of eternal life.

Here the term "circumcision" is used to denote the whole legal system. It does not refer to the institutions of Moses as social and national customs but as forming a way of salvation in place of faith in Christ and his atoning work. To accept the initial rite is to bind oneself to the entire system. "Yea, I testify again to every man that receiveth circumcision, that he is a debtor to do the whole law." Just as the Sacrament of Baptism signifies that a man yields himself wholly to Christ, so circumcision, as a solemn religious rite, would indicate that a man was henceforth under obligation "to do the whole law." It was this decisive step that the Galatians were about to take.

Paul wishes them to see clearly the peril. He would avert the tragedy. "Ye are severed from Christ, ye who would be justified by the law." The word "severed" has a twofold meaning. It means both "to be made nothing," and "to be cut off." The full significance is this: "Ye are made nothing as Christians; ye cease to be Christians; your relations to Christ are canceled." Furthermore, "ye are fallen away from grace." Here "grace" does not mean a spiritual state or course of conduct on the part of a Christian, but the way of salvation which is the free gift of God. To seek to be justified by works of merit is to reject the undeserved favor, the mercy, the redemption, which God freely offers in Christ.

By way of contrast Paul describes the attitude of true believers: "For we through the Spirit by faith wait for the hope of righteousness."

The Holy Spirit is described as the source of Christian hope. This hope is not carnal or fleshly, but it is inspired by the Comforter, the indwelling Spirit of God. Paul elsewhere describes this Spirit as an "earnest of our inheritance," and he declares also that we have been "sealed with the Holy Spirit of promise." On our part, however, this hope rests upon "faith." It is not founded upon our own merit or achievements. The object of this hope is the perfect righteousness which will be ours at the appearing of Christ.

There is no contradiction here to the usual teaching of Paul which indicates that justification is a present experience. This is indeed true, and even now righteousness is both imputed and imparted to the believer. However, faith cherishes the hope of a righteousness far more complete. The aged Paul in his last letter looks to the future and declares, "Henceforth there is laid up for me the crown of righteousness, which the Lord, the righteous judge, shall give me at that day; and not to me only, but also to all them that have loved his appearing." To this future righteousness the Christian is looking forward with keen

and intense expectation. He waits earnestly or eagerly.
It is the crown of all his hopes.

It is, however, as the apostle has intimated, entirely
by faith. When one has come to depend upon Christ he
has no confidence in the flesh, no dependence upon ceremonies or rites which he may perform, "for in Christ
Jesus neither circumcision availeth anything, nor uncircumcision; but faith working through love." Here again
there is no contradiction. Paul has just insisted that
circumcision is the point of departure. It is the sign of an
absolute separation from Christ. Here, on the other hand,
he declares it to be a matter of absolutely no consequence
or significance. The meaning, however, is clear. If circumcision is accepted as a sign and seal that one accepts
the law as a ground of his justification, it is indeed a
serious matter. It severs one from Christ. If, however,
one is "in Christ Jesus," if the will of Christ and the work
of Christ and the law of Christ form the very sphere in
which he lives, then external rites and ceremonies are of
absolutely no concern. They are regarded by the Christian, as they are in fact, of no avail as a means of justification, as a ground of acceptance with God, or as a way of
salvation. For the Christian that way is completely com-
prehended in the simple phrase, "faith working through
love." It is faith alone which is the instrument of salvation. It is a living faith which is expressed in good works,
for it is energetic, living, vital. It works by the law of
love. This coincides with the familiar statement: "Faith
alone justifies, but the faith which justifies is not alone."
It was this familiar truth, this essential teaching of the
gospel of Christ, which was being imperiled in the Galatian churches. (Ch. 5:1-6.)

Paul now turns to deal with those in whom this danger
found its source. "Ye were running well," writes the
apostle. The Galatian Christians had made a noble start
in their Christian lives. They had begun the race with
earnestness and with courage. Who is it then that has

thrown obstacles in their path or has sought to retard them in the race? "Who hindered you that ye should not obey the truth?" The answer to this question is not given. It is not, however, difficult to supply. It seems evident that false teachers had come from Jerusalem. They had denied the authority of Paul and claimed for themselves apostolic power. They had insisted that in addition to faith in Christ the Galatian Christians must observe the entire Mosaic law in order to be accepted by God. These were the Judaizers, the legalists, the false apostles who were working havoc in the Galatian churches and were preventing the Galatians from running the Christian race. Paul insists that "this persuasion came not of him that calleth you." It was God's animating voice that had summoned them to enter the glorious contest and to run for the heavenly prize. Surely, then, any obstacle in the way, any endeavor to turn them aside from the course, could not have its origin in him by whom they had been called. It could come only from those who were ignorant of God or opposing his gracious purposes in Christ. This movement toward ritualism and legalism was no divine movement. It had its inspiration in human ignorance or pride or envy or malice. This perverting influence, this insistence upon the law, was an influence of evil. "A little leaven leaveneth the whole lump," writes the apostle. He is referring either to the doctrine or to the persons of the false teachers. He is quoting a familiar proverb. "Leaven," both in the Old Testament and in the New, is a common symbol. It usually denotes evil whether of character or of influence. Christ warns his followers against "the leaven of the Pharisees and Sadducees" and "the leaven of Herod." Paul quotes the same proverb and urges the Christians in Corinth to "purge out the old leaven" because "our passover also hath been sacrificed, even Christ." He urges his readers to "keep the feast, not with old leaven, neither with the leaven of malice and wickedness, but with the unleavened bread of sincerity and truth" (I Cor. 5:6-8).

In spite of all the evil that is at work in the Galatian churches, Paul expresses his belief that the great majority of believers are still true to him and to the gospel of Christ. He does not wish to implicate all in the weakness and apostasy and sin of the few. "I have confidence to you-ward in the Lord, that ye will be none otherwise minded." Paul feels certain of their loyalty and of their devotion. As to the author of their troubles, however, he cannot escape. God will judge him. As Paul writes, "He that troubleth you shall bear his judgment, whosoever he be." It is not necessary to suppose that Paul has in mind here any particular individual. What he means to say is that whoever may cause trouble, whoever may be the occasion of disturbing the faith of these Christians, will carry the heavy burden of divine condemnation.

Not only had these false teachers been perverting the simple faith of believers, but they had evidently accused Paul of inconsistency and of duplicity. They had been saying that he who was now so opposed to circumcision and to obedience to the Mosaic law was himself preaching circumcision. He had compelled Timothy to submit to the rite. He had himself kept the Feast of Pentecost and taken upon himself Jewish vows. He was a timeserver. In other places and to other Christians he had insisted upon the sacredness of the Jewish law, but among the Galatians he had repudiated this law and its requirements.

Paul asks, as a sufficient reply, this one question: "Why am I still persecuted?" The very reason why these false teachers and others opposed the apostle lay in the fact that he was declaring freedom from the law as a ground of salvation. All his labors, his sufferings, and his distresses could be traced to his fidelity to the gospel of Christ and to his insistence upon justification by faith in him alone. "Then hath the stumblingblock of the cross been done away," adds the apostle. If, indeed, man can be saved by rites and ceremonies, then there is no need of the death of Christ. This painful and ignominious death had been a stumbling block in the way of the Jews. If now salvation depended on Jewish rites and ceremonies, then this stumbling block no longer remained. It is, indeed, a fact that at the foot of the cross we realize the weakness and impotence and worthlessness of our own deeds of righteousness, our own efforts to secure salvation. "For if righteousness is through the law, then Christ died for nought."

Paul could not possibly have been preaching "circumcision" and still have been preaching "the cross." These are symbols of absolutely contradictory and mutually exclusive systems of belief and methods of salvation. One might accept either; he could not hold to both. The first points to the way of works, the second to the way of faith; the first to law, the second to grace; the first to self-righteousness, the second to the righteousness given by God; the first to condemnation, the second to justification and life.

So indignant is the apostle at those who are perverting the gospel of Christ, who are hindering, troubling, and unsettling believers and attacking him with slander, that he cries out in bitterest irony, "I would that they that unsettle you would even go beyond circumcision." He refers to the self-mutilation practiced by the priests of Cybele. His words are not to be taken as the literal expression of a desire. He is speaking with mocking satire. He is expressing with contempt what would be the logical issue of such veneration for the physical rite of circumcision. If his enemies regard it as a way of salvation, they are no better than heathen who put their trust in the observance of even the most debasing ceremonials. The devotees of the Jewish rite may as well go farther and inflict upon themselves all that the pagan cult demands.

One shrinks back from the severe language of the apostle, but one might do well to share something of this righteous indignation at those who today are troubling and

unsettling the church with legalism.   Galatianism is the
most popular heresy of the age.   There are great masses
of Christians to whom religion is a weary round of rites
and ceremonies and duties.   Countless men and women
have been led to believe that salvation is a matter of human achievement.   Many have made an idol of a creed
and are persuaded that the repitition and defense of some
form of words secures acceptance with God and salvation for the soul.

There is need today of calling men back to the cross
and of pointing them toward a living Christ.   Christian
liberty is now imperiled by legalism.   Again there is needed
the great affirmation that "in Christ Jesus neither circumcision availeth anything, nor uncircumcision; but
faith working through love."

B. PERVERTED AS LAWLESSNESS   Ch. 5:13-26

13 For ye, brethren, were called for freedom; only use
*not your freedom for an occasion to the flesh, but through
love be servants one to another.   14 For the whole law is
fulfilled in one word, even in this: Thou shalt love thy
neighbor as thyself.   15 But if ye bite and devour one another, take heed that ye be not consumed one of another.
16 But I say, Walk by the Spirit, and ye shall not fulfil
the lust of the flesh.   17 For the flesh lusteth against the
Spirit, and the Spirit against the flesh; for these are contrary the one to the other; that ye may not do the things
that ye would.   18 But if ye are led by the Spirit, ye are
not under the law.   19 Now the works of the flesh are
manifest, which are* these: *fornication, uncleanness, lasciviousness, 20 idolatry, sorcery, enmities, strife, jealousies,
wraths, factions, divisions, parties, 21 envyings, drunkenness, revellings, and such like; of which I forewarn you,
even as I did forewarn you, that they who practise such
things shall not inherit the kingdom of God.   22 But the
fruit of the Spirit is love, joy, peace, longsuffering, kindness, goodness, faithfulness, 23 meekness, self-control;
against such there is no law.   24 And they that are of Christ*

Jesus have crucified the flesh with the passions and the lusts thereof.

25 If we live by the Spirit, by the Spirit let us also walk. 26 Let us not become vainglorious, provoking one another, envying one another.

It is easy to mistake liberty for license. Men who clamor for freedom are often seeking for anarchy. They wish to do as they please and not to do as they ought. They desire deliverance from all moral restraint. It is not surprising, therefore, that Paul's opposition to legalism was seized upon as an excuse for lawlessness, and that some of his readers were using the doctrines of grace as a justification of self-indulgence and sin.

The apostle found it necessary, therefore, to warn the Galatians that their Christian liberty must not be perverted as license, but must be expressed by obedience to the law of love.

He first reminds them, however, of the reality of their spiritual freedom: "For ye, brethren, were called for freedom." The "ye" is emphatic. It is in contrast to the false teachers who were attempting to bind upon believers the yoke of the Mosaic law. These troublemakers, who were unsettling the Galatian Christians, Paul had bitterly rebuked. By way of contrast he addresses his readers with the tender title of "brethren" and declares that when they were divinely "called" to become followers of Christ, they were thereby destined to enjoy deliverance from legal requirements. They were "called for freedom," or "on the ground of freedom," and with a view to freedom. This spiritual liberty was to be an essential feature of their Christian experience. Its great importance in the mind of the apostle explains the severity with which he rebuked those legalists by whom this freedom was being endangered.

On the other hand, while this liberty must be maintained, it must not be abused. "Only use not your freedom for an occasion to the flesh." The word "only" indicates an anxious fear that this may already be the case or that the temptation is very real. Freedom is their great privilege, but it must not be a shelter for evil. "The flesh," the whole body of sinful impulses which seek to gain control of the will, must not be allowed to find in Christian liberty "an occasion" for wrong action. The knowledge that one is free from the law as a ground of salvation might easily be so abused. This would be the case particularly with those who had been under the restraint of legal requirements. They most of all would be tempted to use their new liberty as "an occasion," a starting point "to the flesh."

To prevent such a false course, Paul insists that there is a law which the most emancipated Christian must obey. It is the law of love. By obedience to this law, all moral requirements would be fulfilled.

It is quite characteristic of the apostle to introduce such a paradox. He has been pleading for liberty; he now insists upon law. He has been reminding Christians of their freedom; he now declares they must be slaves. "Through love be servants one to another."

This apparent contradiction, however, solves the whole problem of the relation between law and gospel, between works and faith, between legalism and Christian liberty. The gospel does not discredit moral law; it shows how this law can be fulfilled. "Faith" does not make "works" unnecessary; it produces "works." Christian liberty does not make one free to sin, but it enables one to attain the righteousness which the law demands. For faith works through love. The gospel, which brings the good news of free grace and pardon, awakens love in the heart toward the Lawgiver, and makes one rejoice to do the will of God as revealed by Christ.

Those who accept the free grace of God in Christ Jesus obey their divine Master, not that they may be saved but because they have been saved. Gratitude and devotion inspire love for God and love for men. And "the whole law is fulfilled in one word, even in this: Thou shalt love thy neighbor as thyself."

It is noticeable that this supreme moral principle is embedded in the very heart of the ancient legal code (Lev. 19:18), and our Lord himself declared that no other rule of action could be more comprehensive, more divine. Christ did not come "to destroy the law . . . but to fulfil." Christ is not opposed to Moses, but, by inspiring love, enables one to obey the law Moses proclaimed. If love rules in the heart, one can work no ill to his neighbor; rather, he will fulfill "the whole law."

The Galatians, however, had not been controlled by this law of love. Turning back to legal requirements and taking their eyes off Christ, and so losing the power of vital faith, they had allowed malice and hatred and bitterness to rule in their hearts. The very controversy aroused by the false teachers had broken out into every possible form of feud and contention. Their conduct toward their fellow Christians could be compared only to the actions of wild beasts. Therefore they are warned, "If ye bite and devour one another, take heed that ye be not consumed one of another." The word "bite" pictures the fierce and cruel manner of their contentions; "devour" indicates the destruction in which these result. Such bitter controversy among Christians will not issue in victory for either party but rather in the utter extinction of the Christian cause.

Whether "the flesh" seeks to manifest itself in immoral license or in angry debate, the Christian must be guarded against its insidious attacks. Paul therefore proceeds to show how the Christian can be victorious in the spiritual conflict in which every soul is engaged.

First of all, and most comprehensive of all, is the exhortation, "Walk by the Spirit, and ye shall not fulfil the lust of the flesh." To "walk" is to pursue one's daily course, to accomplish one's usual tasks, to meet inevitable temptations and duties and sorrows and joys. The entire life of the believer is to be lived "by the Spirit," under his guidance and direction, by his aid and help and power. If a man so lives, he will not yield to sinful desires of the flesh.

Here the term "flesh" refers not merely to bodily appetites. These in themselves may be innocent. The term must include a reference to all evil impulses, examples of which follow in "the works of the flesh" among which are "enmities, strife, jealousies, wraths." The body is the instrument of many evil passions, but "the flesh" indicates the whole being as influenced by wrong affections. It denotes all those tendencies and appetites and dispositions which lead to wrong conduct. Therefore the supremely important secret of moral victory is this: Be fully occupied with activities which are according to the bidding of the Spirit, and you will not yield to the solicitation of "the flesh." If a man is thus occupied with spiritual action, he will be preoccupied against fleshly temptation. This is the familiar principle of "the expulsive power of a higher affection." Victory over the flesh becomes possible if one will "walk by the Spirit."

In the second place, one must be aware of the reality of the conflict. Even in the case of the Christian, and of every Christian, the battle is continuous and full of peril. "The flesh lusteth against the Spirit, and the Spirit against the flesh." In men quite outside the Christian circle, a similar conflict has ever been recognized. The lower impulses in every soul are contending against the higher and seeking to control the will. However, in the case of the believer, the warfare is more severe and the issues are more serious. Here the contestants are not merely the lower and the higher impulses, common to all men; but the very Spirit of God is acting in and through human spirits to ensure victory to those who depend upon his power.

Therefore a Christian is not to suppose that he can escape from the conflict because he has been "born after the Spirit." The old appetites and weaknesses and tendencies remain even in the heart of a true child of God. One who holds any other belief is in imminent moral peril.

On the other hand, one is not to conclude, because his moral conflict is so severe and so continuous, that he therefore is not a Christian. The very fact that he is so conscious of temptation and of struggle is a proof that the Spirit of God is seeking to control his will, and that his conscience has been awakened, and holy desires have been aroused. The greatest saints have the highest ideals and are most sensible of the struggle between flesh and Spirit. They realize that there are abiding forces in the human heart, and that they are in mutual antagonism, "for these are contrary the one to the other." The flesh strives against the control of the Spirit, and the Spirit against the control of the flesh, "that ye may not do the things that ye would."

Paul did not say, as the Authorized Version reads, "Ye cannot do the things that ye would." Either defeat or victory is possible. It is this consciousness of moral conflict and moral peril which is one of the conditions of victory.

In the third place, one is helped to overcome if he remembers his Christian liberty. "If ye are led by the Spirit, ye are not under the law." He is neither under the condemnation of the law nor under bondage to the law.

That is, one is not condemned for the evil impulses which would incline him to evil but only for allowing these to control his will and to be manifest in action. The presence of the "flesh" need cause the Christian neither surprise nor remorse. Evil desire is not a sin unless it is cherished; nor is it true that desire is as evil as the act in which it might result.

Nor is the Christian in bondage to the law. That is, he is not to meet his temptation merely by fixing his thought upon the law he is being solicited to break. Rather, he is to turn to the Christ to whom he belongs and in whom he is given victory. To be absorbed either by the temptation or by the commandment one is inclined to break may invite defeat, but to think of Christ and of his grace and love will enable one to rejoice in true moral freedom.

In the fourth place, victory is made more possible if one realizes the consequences of a victory by the "flesh" or by the "Spirit." With this in view Paul recites "the works of the flesh" and contrasts "the fruit of the Spirit."

"Works," a plural term, may be used to indicate the chaos of riotous vices which are produced by the uncontrolled "flesh"; while "fruit," in the singular number, may intimate the harmonious, united, organic product of the indwelling Spirit.

These "works" are "manifest." They are easily seen and recognized. There is no difficulty in distinguishing between those who "walk by the Spirit" and those who "fulfil the lust of the flesh."

The list of fleshly vices is not complete, but it is comprehensive. Those selected were prevalent in all parts of the Roman Empire and were probably those most common in Galatia. They are pitifully prevalent in all parts of the world today.

It is possible to divide the list as follows: (1) sins of impurity; (2) idolatry; (3) infractions of the law of love; (4) intemperance. The first includes "fornication," "uncleanness," and "lasciviousness," the last of which denotes open and shameless indulgence in impurity.

In the second group are "idolatry" and "sorcery." The former was commonly united in its practices with the vices which precede; while its usual attendant was "sorcery." The latter denotes those forms of magic which ascribe to natural objects supernatural powers and are the result of false views of God and his world.

The third group contains eight of the fifteen "works of the flesh" here enumerated. All have their common origin in a heart devoid of love. "Enmities" are private feuds which may break out in open "strife." "Jealousies" may be secret, but their power is almost limitless, and morally devastating. "Wraths" describe those storms of anger which if uncontrolled become almost demonic. "Factions, divisions, parties" indicate the disturbing, disrupting tendencies of "the flesh" which may destroy the peace of a home, a community, or a church. "Envyings" denote not merely the bitter rivalry of "jealousies," but also the desire to deprive another of his place or possessions and possibly the settled rancor which seeks revenge and often results from the party strife in connection with which it is here named.

The last group of vices includes sins of excess: "drunkenness" and "revellings," which latter term may denote the more open and riotous orgies from which "drunkenness" may result.

As one reads this list of vices it becomes more appalling when one recalls not only that they are prevalent today but that they are "the works of the flesh," and that "the flesh" is active and energetic in the heart of every Christian. Unless one shall "walk by the Spirit," unless one can thus restrain "the flesh," any of these hideous vices may be "manifest" in his own life and conduct. No wonder that Paul adds the solemn warning which he seems to have repeated again and again, "They who practise such things shall not inherit the kingdom of God."

By way of striking contrast there is now arrayed against these fleshly vices a list of Christian virtues, under the term "the fruit of the Spirit." This fruit is one, yet manifold. All these graces spring from a common root. All are the products of a soul which is controlled by the Spirit of Christ.

It is common to divide these graces into three groups, although such a division may be unnecessary and somewhat arbitrary.

First of all stands "love," the queen of the graces. This, with "joy" and "peace," turns the thought toward God. In him these virtues have their source. By him alone they can be maintained. They are not mere human attainments or achievements or qualities. They are "the fruit of the Spirit." "Love is of God"; we "rejoice in the Lord";

"the peace of God" keeps our "hearts and thoughts in Christ Jesus."

The second group of graces directs the attention toward our fellowmen. "Longsuffering" denotes that patient endurance under continual provocation which Paul praises in his hymn of love (I Cor., ch. 13). It bears all things and endures all things; it never fails.

"Kindness" denotes benevolence of disposition. It indicates a desire for the welfare even of those who are continually taxing our patience.

"Goodness" is love in action. It not only desires the welfare of others; it secures that welfare. It is not only benevolence; it is also beneficence.

The last three graces refer more particularly to oneself. "Faithfulness," or fidelity, denotes the quality of a heart which is ever conscious of its own integrity and honesty and sincerity. It is that virtue which ensures loyalty to others and obedience to God. It makes one true to his promise and faithful to his task.

"Meekness" is distinctively a Christian grace. It has not always been regarded as a virtue. It denotes a patient endurance of wrongs, contentedness, quietness, self-effacement. It does not necessarily denote a low conception of one's own abilities, but it is the state of mind which is submissive to the will of God and is unselfish in view of the needs and claims of others. Meekness is not weakness, or mere mildness, or lack of spirit. It requires faith and courage. One may well seek to imitate "the meekness and gentleness of Christ."

"Self-control" is mentioned last. It is, however, by no means the lowest and least of the virtues. The ancient world held it in high repute. Without it even the Christian falls into folly and shame. Self-control implies the rational restraint of all the natural impulses. It may, therefore, well crown the list of virtues which are mentioned in connection with the conflict between "the flesh" and "the Spirit"; for it is exactly this matter of self-control which is especially in mind. If there is to be victory, it can only be as the Spirit of God enables a man to rule his own spirit.

Yet Paul has also been speaking of freedom from the law. Not unnaturally he closes this list of Christian virtues with the statement, "Against such there is no law." Of course there is not. There is surely no law against the exercise of such virtues; but they are the truest fulfillment of the law. This is not a mere platitude. Paul would remind us that the moral law is fulfilled not by a mere human endeavor to produce these graces but by a loving trust in Christ. By his power these virtues can be manifest. Together they form "the fruit of the Spirit."

In the fifth place, victory over the flesh can be secured by regarding "the flesh" as having been once and for all renounced, as belonging to a dead past, and as having no rightful existence in the Christian life. One is to account himself as not under the control of the flesh but as belonging to Christ. For, "they that are of Christ Jesus have crucified the flesh with the passions and the lusts thereof." When we accepted Christ those evil impulses and appetites which sought to control us were regarded as nailed to the cross. In reality they are not dead. They still harass us. They are doomed to death; and to them we need not submit. However, as we oppose them, we, too, feel the bitterness of the cross. It is no easy struggle. Yet we look to the cross of Christ. We see the blackness of sin. We behold him who died for us and ever lives. We turn from the solicitations of the flesh, and in spite of the sense of fierce conflict and conscious weakness we cry, "Thanks be to God, who giveth us the victory through our Lord Jesus Christ."

Death to sin and death with Christ mean a higher life. When we turned from sin and accepted the Lordship of Christ, a new experience began. Therefore, Paul concludes, "If we live by the Spirit, by the Spirit let us also walk." The word for "walk" is not quite the same here

as that used above. There it described the usual daily
life; here the word pictures the activity of one who is making progress on a journey or is pressing toward a goal.

This further help to spiritual victory lies in our effort to
advance toward the likeness of Christ. That is, we are not
to seek merely to overcome the flesh. Such is only a negative attitude. We are to seek positively the attainment
of new virtues. We are not only to avoid the "works of
the flesh"; we are also to endeavor more perfectly to produce the "fruit of the Spirit."

Paul closes the discussion with a reference to the sins
which especially assailed his readers. "Let us not become
vainglorious, provoking one another, envying one another." Whatever our besetting sins may be, let us "walk
by the Spirit" and we shall not "fulfil the lust of the flesh."
We shall find what it is to enjoy true freedom and shall
not allow our Christian liberty to be perverted as license or
to become "an occasion to the flesh."

C. PERFECTED IN LOVE   Ch. 6:1-10

*1 Brethren, even if a man be overtaken in any trespass,
ye who are spiritual, restore such a one in a spirit of gentleness; looking to thyself, lest thou also be tempted. 2 Bear
ye one another's burdens, and so fulfil the law of Christ.
3 For if a man thinketh himself to be something when he
is nothing, he deceiveth himself. 4 But let each man prove
his own work, and then shall he have his glorying in regard
of himself alone, and not of his neighbor. 5 For each man
shall bear his own burden.*

*6 But let him that is taught in the word communicate
unto him that teacheth in all good things. 7 Be not deceived; God is not mocked: for whatsoever a man soweth, that shall he also reap. 8 For he that soweth unto his
own flesh shall of the flesh reap corruption; but he that
soweth unto the Spirit shall of the Spirit reap eternal life.
9 And let us not be weary in well-doing: for in due season
we shall reap, if we faint not. 10 So then, as we have op-*

portunity, let us work that which is good toward all men, and especially toward them that are of the household of the faith.

The spiritual freedom which Paul was defending in this epistle was being endangered by legalism and perverted by license; it should find its true issue and its perfect expression in love. While the apostle has been arguing for liberty, he now asserts that there is a law which every Christian must obey. It is the law of love. Paul proceeds to apply this law in one important sphere of conduct; namely, in the matter of bearing one another's burdens. Of these burdens he specifies two kinds: first, the burdens of moral fault (vs. 1-5) and second, the burdens of temporal needs (vs. 6-10).

The preceding chapter closed with a mention of the vainglorious egotism shown by some who while professing to be Christians were not walking "by the Spirit." Here by way of contrast he sets forth true spiritual conduct, first, in relation to a fallen brother, and second, in relation to religious teachers.

"Brethren," writes the apostle, "even if a man be overtaken in any trespass, ye who are spiritual, restore such a one in a spirit of gentleness." The case which Paul supposes is that of a man who has been discovered in a grievous fault, or, to use a familiar expression, has been "caught red-handed." There is no doubt of his guilt, and the sin is grievous. Even such a man is to be treated with kindness and consideration and with an endeavor for his spiritual good.

There are those who understand the word "overtaken" in a different sense. They take it to mean that the offender has been surprised by some sudden temptation. He has yielded to temper or passion and thus unexpectedly has fallen. However, this would rather minimize the guilt and the seriousness of the offense. It is more probable that Paul intended to emphasize the fault of the offender and to say that even such a conspicuous failure should not prevent his fellow Christians from showing him sympathy and aid. When the apostle says, "Ye who are spiritual, restore such a one," some understand him to be speaking with irony. More probably by the term "spiritual" he is pointing back to the previous chapter where he has been insisting that if we "walk by the Spirit" we "shall not fulfil the lust of the flesh." He is intimating that, for those who are so walking, an opportunity is given of showing their true spiritual character by the sympathetic help of the one who has been guilty of the moral lapse. The effort should be not merely to "restore such a one" to his place in the Christian circle, but rather, to secure for him that inner spiritual recovery which the word probably pictures, a word which is used in the New Testament to describe the mending of a net or the setting of a limb. It should be the aim of the spiritually minded Christian to place an offending brother in a position of moral health.

Such an action requires "a spirit of gentleness." Only one who has this disposition or temper can undertake so delicate and difficult a task. It requires meekness and sympathy and kindness of a very high order to be a spiritual physician, or to lead back into a path of virtue one who has gone astray.

The chief hindrances to such a blessed ministry are pride and self-conceit. In order that such barriers may be removed, Paul urges the spiritual Christian to consider his own weaknesses and possible shortcomings. He uses the singular instead of the plural number, indicating that each one should so regard himself in order that by true humility he may be able to restore the one who has sinned. "Looking to thyself, lest thou also be tempted."

Paul then gives the general exhortation which would cover all such particular cases: "Bear ye one another's burdens, and so fulfil the law of Christ." The burdens which Paul therefore has specially in mind are the burdens of moral fault. Perhaps none are so pathetic, none press so heavily on the soul, as the burdens of detected sin and conscious shame.

The exhortation should not be limited to burdens of this specific kind, yet these are the hardest to endure and are the most difficult to lift from other hearts or even to share helpfully. To lighten such burdens is an act of truest love. It is thus possible to "fulfil the law of Christ." This was "the law" which Christ himself obeyed. It was the law which he required of his followers. Obedience to it is the true sign of the Christian.

In order further to remove the pride and vainglory which might prevent obedience to this law, the apostle intimates the peril of self-conceit which is usually due to self-deception. "For if a man thinketh himself to be something when he is nothing, he deceiveth himself." He surely deceives no one else. Yet it is possible for a man to have so high a regard for his own virtue and moral excellence that he may have altogether an erroneous and false estimate of himself. This wrong impression is heightened by comparing himself with the fallen brother. In contrast to such weakness and obvious imperfection, a man may pride himself upon his own moral attainment. Instead of exulting in such a comparison, Paul urges each man to test his own work in the light of his conscious obligations. He probably then will have very little reason for self-congratulation. His course of action, however, may stand the test of such careful scrutiny, and if so, he rightly may find in it a ground of satisfaction. Or, as the apostle says, "Let each man prove his own work, and then shall he have his glorying in regard of himself alone" and not by comparison with "his neighbor."

Thus it is in the light of his own responsibility to God that a man should test his life and character, "for each man shall bear his own burden." The burden to which Paul here refers is, therefore, the burden of moral responsibility. This no man can shirk and no man can share. With this in view the apparent contradiction disappears.

The apostle had said, "Bear ye one another's burdens," and he now declares that "each man shall bear his own burden." Both statements are absolutely true, and when one remembers the latter, namely, the great weight of responsibility for right-doing which rests upon him as a Christian, and when he realizes how far short he has fallen of any standard of perfection, he will then be the more ready, in a spirit of gentleness, to bear his brother's burdens of fault and of weakness and thus to "fulfil the law of Christ."

There are, however, burdens of a different character which the spiritual man will seek to share. Among these may be mentioned the heavy load of temporal necessities which rests on the teachers of religion, as indeed it does on all men. It would seem that these leaders of the Galatian church had been neglected or that the members of the church had failed to show them due consideration and sympathy. Therefore the apostle gives the injunction, "Let him that is taught in the word communicate unto him that teacheth in all good things." It is evident, therefore, that in the early church and here among the first Christian converts there were officers whose duty it was to give instruction in the gospel, to explain and enforce the Christian message, to teach "the word." It is also evident that the Christian community was expected to support these officers by voluntary gifts. The "good things" which the "taught" were to share with the teacher are not to be limited in meaning to a salary or to a financial recompense, but they surely include this, and it is probable that such is the first meaning of the phrase in this passage. Paul was ever ready to defend the principle that one who preached the gospel should be given financial support by those for whom he labored. In writing to the Corinthians he laid stress upon the fact that he himself had been willing to forego this right, but a right it was which usually should be claimed. In this connection he used a familiar figure of speech in which he stated that the expectation of financial recompense for preaching the gospel was as natural as the expectation of a husbandman to reap the fruit of his labor. "He that ploweth ought to plow in hope," Paul had written, "and he that thresheth, to thresh in hope of partaking. If we sowed unto you spiritual things, is it a great matter if we shall reap your carnal things?"

Here, in writing to the Galatians, he employs the same figure of sowing and reaping. Its application, however, is somewhat different. Here he is intimating that selfish and unsympathetic and unjust dealings with ministers of the gospel cannot but result in a harvest of spiritual meagerness and leanness. But, on the other hand, generous dealings with religious leaders will result in the spiritual growth and enrichment of the Christian community. As to this the Galatians should not deceive themselves. They could not defy such a divinely established law.

Paul states this truth, however, by enunciating a universal principle: "Be not deceived; God is not mocked: for whatsoever a man soweth, that shall he also reap." This law of the harvest is familiar; but it is a law of which no one should have the slightest doubt. A man should not deceive himself, much less can he with impunity deceive God, that is, by managing to escape the consequences of his acts. "God is not mocked." The word here is so picturesque that we find it impossible to translate it without apparent irreverence. It describes the impudent expression or gesture of a man who openly shows his contempt of a person whom he has deceived. When a man attempts to avoid the results of his own moral action, he is really showing such contempt for God. It is utterly impossible for a man to escape the harvest which springs from the seeds which his own deeds have sown.

There are those who feel that they have escaped the results of immoral conduct if they have been able to conceal from the world their wrongdoing. Others seem to imagine that if the wrong is merely forgotten and regarded as a matter of the past there will be no harvest of suffering or pain. Still others seem to imagine that religion is a device intended to secure immunity from the results of moral fault. Men deceive themselves by believing that the paying of penance or the confession of a fault to a priest or minister will prevent a wrong course of action from producing any distressing consequences. They even believe that the saying of masses or prayers will enable a gross sinner to escape from purgatory into paradise. Others suppose that the asking and the receiving of the forgiveness of God will cause this law of sowing and reaping to be suspended. There is a reality in pardon, but it does not prevent the sinner from reaping a harvest of punishment and of shame. It does secure this supremely important thing; namely, the removal of the barrier of conscious guilt which separates the soul from God. It does bring one again into fellowship with the loving Father whose heart has been offended. It does enable one with more patience and submission to bear the burden which the fault has brought upon the sinning soul. It does also prevent one from sowing further seed which might result in a greater and more pitiful harvest of sorrow and distress. However, the consequences cannot be averted. "He that soweth unto his own flesh shall of the flesh reap corruption."

By "the flesh" is here meant the impulses and tendencies of human nature unrenewed by the Spirit of God and opposed to the will of God. It describes not merely bodily appetites, but all those dispositions and impulses which are wrong, which may indeed spring from fleshly desire and may use the body as their instrument; but the text includes those attitudes and inclinations of the mind which impel a man to selfishness, to forgetfulness of others, and to disregard of God. The actions which result from "the flesh" cannot fail to result in moral weakness and in sinful transgression. The result must be "corruption." This is a strange description of a harvest, but it is tragically true. Even the body is affected by a wrong course of action, and eternity itself cannot limit the results upon the soul of such continued conduct. There must be repentance and pardon and new power for self-control and self-discipline. This can be secured by fellowship with Christ and by dependence upon his grace. He can bring good out of evil. He can secure a harvest of abiding beauty and joy.

"He that soweth unto the Spirit shall of the Spirit reap eternal life." It is this more glorious aspect of the truth upon which Paul especially dwells. The whole intent of the passage is not so much to warn as to encourage. The harvest of corruption is not more real than the harvest of eternal life. To sow to the Spirit is to cherish those impulses and practice those activities which are in accordance with the promptings and guidance of the indwelling Spirit of Christ. The phrase describes the daily life and conduct and actions of those who "walk by the Spirit" (ch. 5:16), and "live by the Spirit" (v. 25). The issues of such living are pictured here by a term which does not mean merely endless existence. Such an existence is as true of the evil as of the good. However, "eternal life" indicates not merely the continuance of existence but a certain kind of existence. It denotes that life which is produced in the soul by the Spirit of God as one puts his trust in the Son of God and allows his Spirit to produce in him the peaceable fruits of righteousness. This life is a present possibility and enjoyment, but it expands through all the ages to come and enables a man to develop more and more into the likeness of Christ himself.

It is with such a superb promise that Paul gives his closing exhortation: "Let us not be weary in well-doing: for in due season we shall reap, if we faint not." His first reference may have been to the generous support of the Christian ministry, but he is, of course, speaking here in unrestricted terms. No matter what the well-doing may be, whether it is bearing one another's burdens of fault or of finance, whether it is relieving those in physical distress or in moral need, whether it is sharing with others our wealth or our sympathy, we can be absolutely sure of a great and beauteous harvest "if we faint not." The word "faint" describes the action of the laborer who, when toiling in the harvest field, withdraws in weakness and in discouragement. Let us continue our sowing even though it is with tears and with an aching heart. Let us be sure that we shall yet come with rejoicing, bringing our sheaves with us. "So then, as we have opportunity, let us work that which is good toward all men, and especially toward them that are of the household of the faith." We have opportunity for well-doing. A time and a possibility for such kindly action are always present. Let us then be faithful while the opportunity lasts. It is true that we should be especially mindful of the great family of believers to which we belong. There are some duties which we owe specifically to our fellow Christians and to those who hold offices of spiritual oversight, but there is no limiting to any one circle. Our kindness should extend as widely as our influence, and in all our dealings we should show that the liberty which we enjoy in Christ is manifested by a continual observance of the divine law of love.

V
THE CONCLUSION
Ch. 6:11-18

Paul regards the concluding paragraph of his letter as of great importance. He seems to take the pen from the hand of the scribe, and in large bold characters to write his final words. It was his custom to dictate his letters to an amanuensis and to write only his signature at the close to authenticate the message. Some have thought that this entire epistle to the Galatians was written by the hand of the apostle. It is more probable that it is to these closing sentences that he refers when he says, "See with how large letters I write unto you with mine own hand." The size of the characters which Paul employs may indicate the importance of the message which these characters express. It may be like writing a sentence in capital letters or underscoring it, or like other modern devices adopted for the sake of emphasis. Some, however, believe that the size of these letters was due to Paul's imperfect eyesight. They think that his custom of dictating to a scribe was due to his impaired vision, and the suggestion is made that these large characters add a pathetic touch to this letter, calling to mind the infirmity of the writer. Whichever view is taken, there can be little doubt that Paul lays great stress upon these closing words.

Like the introduction, this conclusion forms an epitome of the epistle. Its three sections, which are closed with the benediction, correspond to the three great divisions of the letter. The order, however, is reversed. In the last two chapters of the epistle, Paul has been warning his readers against the Judaizers who would rob them of their liberty; so in the first sentences of this conclusion he pauses to rebuke these Judaizers and to expose their duplicity. (Vs. 11-13.) The central chapters of the epistle are concerned with the doctrine of justification by faith. So in the central section of this conclusion (vs. 14-16) Paul states that his own expectation of salvation is based upon the cross of Christ and the new life which is imparted through faith in him. The last sentence of this concluding message (v. 17) corresponds to the two chapters which open the epistle and which establish Paul's apostolic authority. Here he declares that his relationship to Christ, his devotion, and his authority are at once evidenced by the marks which he bears on his body of the sufferings which he has endured in the service of his Lord.

A. A REBUKE TO THE LEGALISTS   Ch. 6:11-13

11 See with how large letters I write unto you with mine own hand. 12 As many as desire to make a fair show in the flesh, they compel you to be circumcised; only that they may not be persecuted for the cross of Christ. 13 For not even they who receive circumcision do themselves keep the law; but they desire to have you circumcised, that they may glory in your flesh.

As Paul turns his attention to the false teachers who have so troubled the Galatian church and to those believers who may have been misled by them, he makes a severe charge of insincerity, of duplicity, and of inconsistency. Those, he says, who are seeking to compel the Galatians to adopt the Mosaic ritual are inspired only by selfish and cowardly motives. "As many as desire to make a fair show in the flesh, they compel you to be circumcised." Their desire is to win favor with men or to avoid the loss of popularity or position. They wish to escape the persecution to which all followers of Christ are being subjected. The desire of these leaders is "that they may not be persecuted for the cross of Christ." To make a show of their zeal for the law of Moses would possibly protect them from the hostility of the Jews and enable them, while still trusting in Christ, to avoid suffering for the sake of Christ.

Then, too, these men are insincere. "For not even they who receive circumcision do themselves keep the law." They were evidently inconsistent in their living, and while pretending to be zealous for legal observances, they were failing to bear in their own lives the burdensome restriction of the law.

They were seeking only to secure the submission of their fellow Christians in order that they might make a great show of their zeal for Judaism by winning Gentiles to submission to Jewish ritual. In all ages even those who are most bitter and zealous as partisans are frequently impelled not by devotion to the truth but by selfish motives, by a desire for prominence, by fear of persecution, and by an eagerness to win the favor of men.

B. PAUL'S CONFIDENCE IN THE CROSS
Ch. 6:14-16

14 But far be it from me to glory, save in the cross of our Lord Jesus Christ, through which the world hath been crucified unto me, and I unto the world. 15 For neither is circumcision anything, nor uncircumcision, but a new creature. 16 And as many as shall walk by this rule, peace be upon them, and mercy, and upon the Israel of God.

In contrast with the selfish and insincere legalists who found their glory in securing followers whom they could compel to submit to Jewish rites, Paul made his boast in the cross of Christ and in the new life granted by his Spirit. "Far be it from me to glory, save in the cross of our Lord Jesus Christ." The cross is a strange thing in which to rejoice or to boast. It is the symbol of ignominy, shame, death. The cross of Christ is of all other crosses the strangest cause for joy. It is the cross of the only pure and sinless man who ever lived. Why does Paul glory in this cross?

It is because of what it has secured for him and because of the new life which has resulted from faith in Christ. By this cross, Paul declares, "the world hath been crucified unto me, and I unto the world." The "world" to which he refers must be, first of all and chiefly, the whole world of Jewish rites and ceremonies. Paul has identified himself with Christ and he has found that the death of Christ is itself sufficient for those who put their trust in him to secure pardon for sin and acceptance with God. To this finished work of Christ, Paul need and can add nothing. Therefore, to him the whole sphere of ceremonies and rites has lost all attraction. It appears to him as something dead and crucified. So, also, it has lost all claims upon him. He has been crucified to the world. To one who has accepted Christ as his Redeemer, religious ceremonies in themselves are no longer a ground of glorying or a basis of hope. "For neither is circumcision anything [in itself], nor uncircumcision, but a new creature." This new life which results from faith in Christ is Paul's chief and only concern. His boast and his glory are in the cross and in the fact that through Christ he has become a new creature. "As many as shall walk by this rule," he adds, "peace be upon them, and mercy, and upon the Israel of God." The "rule" to which Paul alludes is the great principle which he has just stated. It is the rule of those who place their whole confidence for acceptance with God upon his redeeming work in Christ, and whose great joy is found in the power of holy living which is granted them by the Spirit of Christ. Upon such believers Paul invokes the peace of God and the mercy of God.

When he adds "And upon the Israel of God," he does not indicate a second class of believers; he is indicating all who put their trust in Christ. They are the true "Israel"; they are the spiritual descendants of Abraham and of Jacob. The very word is in itself a rebuke to the Galatian heresy. Those converts were being tempted to believe that the true "heirs of the promise" were the Christians who might also adopt the Mosaic ritual. Paul insists that the true spiritual Israel consists of those who glory in the cross and in the power of the risen Christ.

C. THE MARKS OF AN APOSTLE   Ch. 6:17

17 Henceforth let no man trouble me; for I bear branded on my body the marks of Jesus.

There were three classes of persons in the ancient world who were branded on their bodies: soldiers, slaves, and devotees. Paul declares that on his body there are "the marks of Jesus." He refers, of course, to the scars which had been left by the scourgings and stonings and vigils and toils which he had endured for the sake of Christ. They prove that he belongs to Christ. The apostle is here pointing us back to the early chapters of his epistle where he is arguing as to his apostolic authority. He is now intimating that there should be no doubt as to his relation to Jesus. The scars on his body indicate that he belongs wholly to his Master. He is his soldier; he is his slave; he is his devotee. This last use of this word described those temple slaves who were branded to indicate that they belonged to a certain god, or that they had adopted a certain cult as their own. The Galatian Christians were tempted to adopt outward signs as indicating their religious status. Paul declares that his brands of suffering and of shame point to the living Lord for whom he has endured all things and to whom he belongs. In view of such a relationship he exclaims with something of impatience, "Henceforth let no man trouble me." He will not again undertake to deal with those puerile yet vexatious attacks which have been made upon his sincerity and upon his apostolic authority. He sets them aside once and for all with this appeal which should be final: "I bear branded on my body the marks of Jesus." His assailants should henceforth leave him in peace.

D. THE BENEDICTION   Ch. 6:18

18 The grace of our Lord Jesus Christ be with your spirit, brethren. Amen.

This closing sentence, this last word of farewell, is familiar yet in a sense unique. Its main and inclusive petition is for "the grace of our Lord Jesus Christ." Grace is unmerited favor. It has been shown supremely in and through the mission and work of Christ. It stands opposed to all the works of the "flesh" and all dependence upon self for salvation.

This prayer, therefore, rightly concludes the letter in which Paul has been warning his readers against any return to ceremony and ritual as a ground of acceptance with God. He asks that this unmerited favor which has been shown them through Christ may be multiplied. He prays that the pardon which they have received may be followed by power for holy living, and that the very Spirit of God may dwell in their hearts, moving upon their spirits and enabling them to live as heirs of God and as joint heirs with Christ.

A final delicate touch is found in the last word of his petition. It is the word "brethren." A reader may have at times supposed that Paul's severity had made him forget the true relation which he sustained to his disciples in Galatia. This last syllable indicates that the apostle does not regard his readers with anger or enmity. He does not think of them last of all even as his pupils and followers. He reminds them that they and he are all one in Christ Jesus, heirs of the same promise, recipients of the same grace. They have been saved by faith, and his whole desire is that they may maintain their position as Christian brethren, not as servants of the law but as free heirs of the grace of God.